WAR IN
ECOLOGICAL
PERSPECTIVE

WAR IN ECOLOGICAL PERSPECTIVE

PERSISTENCE, CHANGE, AND ADAPTIVE PROCESSES
IN THREE OCEANIAN SOCIETIES

By
Andrew P. Vayda

Cook College, Rutgers University

Plenum Press · New York and London

Library of Congress Cataloging in Publication Data

Vayda, Andrew Peter.
  War in ecological perspective.

  Includes bibliographical references and index.
  1. Ethnology – Oceanica. 2. War. 3. Human ecology. I. Title.
  GN663.V38   301.6'334   75-40272
  ISBN 0-306-30876-2

© 1976 Plenum Press, New York
A Division of Plenum Publishing Corporation
227 West 17th Street, New York, N.Y. 10011

United Kingdom edition published by Plenum Press, London
A Division of Plenum Publishing Company, Ltd.
Davis House (4th Floor), 8 Scrubs Lane, Harlesden, London, NW10 6SE, England

Printed in the United States of America

To Yombran, old warrior and friend.

PREFACE

This book deals with war in three Oceanian societies. More specifically, it analyzes the following: the process of war in relation to population pressure among New Guinea's Maring people; extension and contraction in the headhunting activities of the Iban people of Sarawak during the nineteenth century; and the disruption resulting from the introduction of muskets in the warfare of the Maoris of New Zealand. In all of the analyses, I have viewed war as a process rather than simply as something that either does or does not occur and I have tried to see how the process relates to environmental problems or perturbations actually faced by people. The use of such an approach can, I believe, lead to important understandings about war and, more generally, about how people respond to environmental problems. A goal in this book is to show that this is so.

Although it is only relatively recently that the significance of viewing war as a process became clear to me, my interest in war in relation to environmental and demographic phenomena is of long standing. The beginning of the studies resulting in the present book can, in fact, be said to date back to the mid-1950s when I was in New Zealand to do library research for my Ph.D. dissertation on Maori warfare. Subsequently, while at the University of British Columbia from 1958 to 1960 and in London during the summer of 1960, I began to delve into the historical material on Sarawak and the Ibans to make comparisons between the Maoris and Ibans in their warfare and ecology. Field research in the Maring region of New Guinea in 1962 to 1963 and again in 1966 enabled me to obtain data—through interviews and observation—in a society where a traditional war process had still been operating shortly before my arrival. Following the New Guinea field trips, I undertook analysis of the Maring data and resumed library research on the Maoris and Ibans. This work was done mainly at Columbia and Rutgers universities. Brief visits to Sarawak in 1974 and again in 1975 made it possible for me to obtain some additional information about the Ibans.

In the course of these years of research, help in various forms was received from many people and institutions—too many to be mentioned here. Grateful acknowledgments of their contributions have been made in my other publications, listed in the bibliographies at the end of the present book. Not previously acknowledged, however, is certain help received specifically for the preparation of this book. Therefore I extend my thanks here to the following: the Rutgers University Research Council, for funds for manuscript preparation; Cherry Lowman, for providing the photograph from which Plate 4 has been prepared; Ulla Wagner and Björn Ranung of the University of Stockholm, for permission to use the Sarawak maps which Dr. Ranung prepared for Dr. Wagner's book, *Colonialism and Iban Warfare*, published in Stockholm in 1972; Peter M. Kedit, Ethnologist, Sarawak Museum, for arranging to have these maps redrawn (so as to indicate the new divisions and new division boundaries of Sarawak) and for providing the photographic prints from which Plates 7–9 have been prepared; Dorothy Urlich Cloher, for sending me two maps that she prepared for her M.A. thesis, *The Distribution and Migrations of the North Island Maori Population about 1800–1840* (University of Auckland, 1969) and for

giving me permission to reproduce the maps (Plates 10 and 13);
William C. Clarke, for sending me—and permitting me to reproduce—the map (Plate 1) which he and Ian Heyward prepared
originally for my article, "Phases of the Process of War and Peace
among the Marings of New Guinea," *Oceania* **42:** 1–24, September
1971; the editors of *Oceania*, for permission to reprint portions of
that article in Chapter 2 of the present book; the editors of *Annual
Review of Ecology and Systematics*, for permission to reprint, in
Chapters 1, 2, and 5, portions of my article, "Warfare in Ecological
Perspective," *Annual Review of Ecology and Systematics*, **5:** 183–193,
1974; the Academy of Political Science, for permission to use as
Chapter 4 a revised version of an article originally published as
"Maoris and Muskets in New Zealand: Disruption of a War Sys-
tem" in *Political Science Quarterly* **85:** 560–584, December 1970; and
the New York Times Company, for permission to reprint, in
Chapter 3, Note 11, the quotation from Shane Stevens' article on
"The 'Rat Packs' of New York."

Andrew P. Vayda

Somerset, New Jersey
February, 1976

CONTENTS

LIST OF PLATES

1

INTRODUCTION

So-called conflict theorists and the many scholars who have asked
about the causes of war have seldom looked at war as a process.
Instead they have generally accepted, implicitly or explicitly, a simple dichotomy between war and peace. One author, reviewing contributions to the *Journal of Conflict Resolution* during the years 1957–
1968, has remarked: "I get the feeling that, for most *JCR* contributors,
once a war happens, it ceases to be interesting" (Converse, 1968:476–
477). Commenting on this, a historian has suggested that conflict
theorists' neglect of the dynamics of war may reflect a prevalent
notion that "once a war breaks out, its end is inherent in its beginning—simply a mindless, inescapable playing-out of forces set in
motion at the outset . . . " (Carroll, 1970:15). Even with the kind of
awareness of escalation that has been forced upon all of us by the
recent example of the development of small wars into a larger one in
Southeast Asia, the literature on escalation remains, as remarked by

1

the editors of a book on *Theory and Research on the Causes of War,* "quite scanty" (Pruitt and Snyder, 1969:57).

It is my belief that viewing war as not simply something that either does or does not occur, but rather as a process, can lead to important understandings—both about war and, more generally, about how people respond to environmental problems or perturbations. It is this belief that led to the decision to bring together here three case studies dealing with Oceanian societies with which I have become familiar through either anthropological field work or historical research. In the case studies, war is viewed as a process and its relation to environmental problems or perturbations is explored.

Viewing war as a process consisting of recurrent, distinguishable phases enables us to ask questions different from those usual in studies of war. We can ask not only about the conditions conducive to the outbreak of war but also about those conducive to escalation from one phase of war processes to another. We can ask not only about the inevitability of war but also about the inevitability of escalation. We can ask about the duration and frequency not simply of warfare but rather of particular phases of war processes. And we can ask about the relation of the temporal and other properties of war processes to the problems or perturbations that the processes may be responding to. All of these are, in fact, questions with which we will be dealing in the succeeding chapters.

As will be made clear, exploring the relation of war processes to environmental problems or perturbations is what I regard as looking at war in an ecological perspective. It is appropriate therefore to indicate briefly that this is different from two other kinds of enterprises involving attempts to relate warfare to environmental factors.

One of these is the search for a single environmental or ecological cause of warfare either in all societies or in some broad category of them. This search is based on the assumption that war may be usefully regarded as a discrete phenomenon for which there must be a specifiable, discrete cause or set of causes. To those who, like myself, see the world as composed of continuous processes and feedback systems in which many "causes" operate simultaneously and are not clearly separable from effects (cf. Hubbell, 1973:95), this assumption and, concomitantly, the enterprise based on it seem ill-advised. Among examples of what the search for a single environmental or ecological cause of warfare has produced so far are statements to the effect that population pressure is the underlying or principal cause of warfare in "primitive" or "barbarous" societies or even in human societies in general (Harris, 1971:227, 228; Harris, 1972; Krzywicki, 1934:Chap. 4; Newcomb, 1950; Thompson, 1929:4–5). These statements have received empirical refutation in the form of evidence that war occurs when appreciable population pressure is absent and when none of the belligerents either needs or seeks more land or other resources (Bremer et al., 1973; Fathauer, 1954; Murphy, 1970:166; Sauvy, 1969:520–522). While population pressure is a major concern of the case studies in the succeeding chapters, it will be seen that no claim for its causal primacy is made.

Another enterprise involving consideration of environmental or ecological factors is the attempt to discover the origins of human aggression and warfare. This has led to such currently popular interpretations as Robert Ardrey's, whereby human aggression and warfare are seen as originating in (and persisting from) the hunting and meat-eating adaptations made by our primate ancestors to conditions of drought in Pliocene times (Ardrey, 1961). This is not the place for any extensive criticism of Ardrey's interpretations or of the similar views set forth by Konrad Lorenz (1966) and others. (An anthology of critiques of these views is available [Montagu, 1973].) Suffice it to say that in looking at war in an ecological perspective we will not be content to use the perspective only for events that happened millions of years ago. Instead we will be asking questions about the place of warfare in people's systemic responses to perturbations much more recent than the droughts of the Pliocene. This means, among other things, that we will be considering the possibility that some recent warfare has operated within adaptive systems and has not been simply an expression of genetically programmed drives uselessly or deleteriously persisting from much earlier times.

The perturbations with which the case studies in the succeeding chapters happen to be mainly concerned are those associated with population pressure. However, as mentioned, I am interested in using material from the studies for raising general questions about perturbations and the processes responding to them. More has to be said about this.

Ideally, the case studies would include some that are focussed on perturbations other than those associated with population pressure and on response processes other than those involving warfare. Unfortunately, I have not yet completed any such case studies, whereas I have, for more than fifteen years, been doing research on war as waged by particular societies in relation to demographic and/or ecological problems. When this research began, my general objectives, in accord with those prevalent among ecologists, were to identify mechanisms whereby the size of human populations is adjusted to the carrying capacities of their environments and to show how these mechanisms operate. A more specific objective was to see whether warfare, which some other anthropologists were then interpreting in relation to people's purported needs for tension release and social cohesion (see Vayda, 1961a:346–347), was, by virtue of its effects on mortality and the dispersion of populations, one of the mechanisms operating among some primitive societies to adjust the size of populations to the available resources. My research to date on warfare, land use, and population movements among the Marings of New Guinea, the Ibans of Borneo, and the Maoris of New Zealand has, in fact, contributed to meeting these objectives, and readers who are so inclined can regard the chapters to follow as reports on the extent to which the objectives have been met. It can, I think, be claimed that the materials presented do indicate an important role for warfare in the maintenance of man/resource balances among the three peoples studied.

There are, however, other peoples whose warfare does not seem to be related to the maintenance of man/resource balances, and, in the case of some societies, the maintenance of such balances is achieved, not by warfare, but rather by various other devices including migrations, trade, infanticide, and intensification of land use (see the discussion in Wright, 1965:Chap. 31). The fact of such alternatives to warfare is in accord with what is sometimes described as the "principle of multiple solutions for adaptational problems in evolution," paralleled by the sociological concepts of "functional alternatives" and "functional equivalents" (Hempel, 1959:285; cf. Collins and Vayda, 1969). Different human populations, just like different animal populations (Colinvaux, 1973:Chap. 36; Force, 1974:624), are regulated by different factors. There cannot be anything surprising in this to anybody who has been duly impressed that cultural evolution, much like biological evolution as described in George Gaylord Simpson's classic discussion of the subject (1949:Chap. 4), is opportunistic—that the changes the process comprises occur "as they may and not as would be hypothetically best" and are constrained by the structures and mechanisms which the adapting individuals and populations already possess. (For some discussion of parallels between cultural and biological evolution in this respect, see Vayda and Rappaport, 1968:486–487.)

Moreover, in the years since the research reported here was begun, we have become increasingly aware that the maintenance of man/resource balances is not equally a problem for all peoples and that assumptions such as are still made by some anthropologists (e.g., Cook, 1972:25; Dumond, 1972:287; Harris, 1971:224–225; Smith and Young, 1972:33) to the effect that human populations always tend to expand to the limits imposed by the carrying capacity of their environments may not be justified. In other words, particular populations, such as some of those noted by anthropologists in recent articles or books critical of the old assumptions (e.g., Douglas, 1966, and Wilkinson, 1973a, 1973b), may have stabilized well below the environmental limits and may thus have made themselves, whether deliberately or not, less liable to be disrupted by environmental changes adversely affecting carrying capacities.[1] George Cowgill, an archeologist, has put it as follows:

> . . . we cannot take it for granted that inelastic human population growth rates characteristically drive population densities up to the level where significant stress due to resource shortages is experienced or seen as an imminent threat. . . . Undoubtedly there have been *some* instances of ancient societies that experienced problems of actual or imminent overpopulation. But we cannot take this as a given. Most societies most of the time do not seem to have had overpopulation problems, and if some societies some of the time have had these problems, then the reasons are not self-evident, but are a matter for investigation. (Cowgill, 1975:513–514)

The foregoing is consistent with what I would now regard as appropriate procedures for studying how people respond to environmental problems or perturbations. Instead of starting with the assumption that all populations have to contend with the same problems (whether these be problems of overpopulation or whatever), we need to find out what problems particular populations actually are or have been confronted with. Having done this, we can proceed to study the processes employed in responding to those problems. In the case of the three societies discussed in the pages to follow, the available evidence is not as abundant and unequivocal as one might wish it to be, but population pressure and associated stress can nevertheless reasonably be identified as problems that members of the societies have had, at least sometimes, to deal with and the war processes can be seen as operating partly in response to those problems. This does not mean, however, that I would deny the importance of other problems, whether for the societies treated here or for other ones, or that I would not be interested in the actual processes, whether warlike or not, involved in the responses to those problems. A program of looking at warfare or at any other process in ecological perspective is not regarded here as a search for some universal environmental cause of the process. What the program calls for instead is asking how the process in question relates to the particular environmental problems faced by the population under study.[2]

To some anthropologists, this might sound like a call to return to something like the particularism—the "programmatic avoidance of theoretical syntheses" (Harris, 1968:250)—associated with the Boasian period in American anthropology. If this were indeed what is being advocated here, it would be hard to reconcile with my professed concern for raising general questions about perturbations and the processes responding to them. There is, however, no real contradiction. On the one hand, we may want to reject population pressure and warfare as categories or variables to be included in generalizations of broad scope and applicability. On the other hand, we can still aim, as I have suggested elsewhere (Vayda, 1974), to raise general questions and to develop generalizations in terms of such variables as the magnitude, duration, and novelty of perturbations, the magnitude and reversibility of responses to them, the temporal order in which responses of different magnitudes occur, and the persistence or nonpersistence of response processes.[3] The generalizations will be about the relation between perturbations and responses, and we will need to base them on observations of particular cases of perturbations and responses, such as population pressure and war processes among the societies treated in this book. Thus, generalizations such as are to be suggested later in the book about the temporal ordering of response processes (so that overexpenditures of resources in response to minor or transitory perturbations are avoided) need to be based on specific observations about, for example, how the antecedents of territorial conquests among the Ibans were localized headhunting raids in response to misfortunes that had increased as the result of population pressure.

It is possible that some readers looking at the case studies will be interested only in the specific observations about warfare and land use. The succeeding chapters can certainly be read simply as accounts of warfare as practiced by three non-Western societies. I hope, however, that most readers will find more in the chapters and that they will become persuaded of the value of viewing war as a process and will want to join in a program of raising questions and developing generalizations about perturbations and responses and about the conditions conducive to either the persistence or the breakdown of response processes.

WAR AS A PROCESS
The Maring Case

To show the possibility and desirability of viewing war as a process, we can turn first to the Maring people of the Bismarck Mountains of eastern New Guinea. A multiphase war process operating among these people will be described and analyzed in this chapter. The concluding section of the chapter will indicate the features of the Maring process that are especially important for understanding how war processes in general can operate adaptively in relation to perturbations that people must deal with.

THE MARING REGION AND PEOPLE

The Maring region (see Plate 1) is used here as the designation for a rugged, forested area of about 190 square miles within which live some 7,000 people sharing certain cultural characteristics and speaking the Maring language.[1] Cutting across the region is the Bismarck Range, flanked by the Simbai River to the north and the

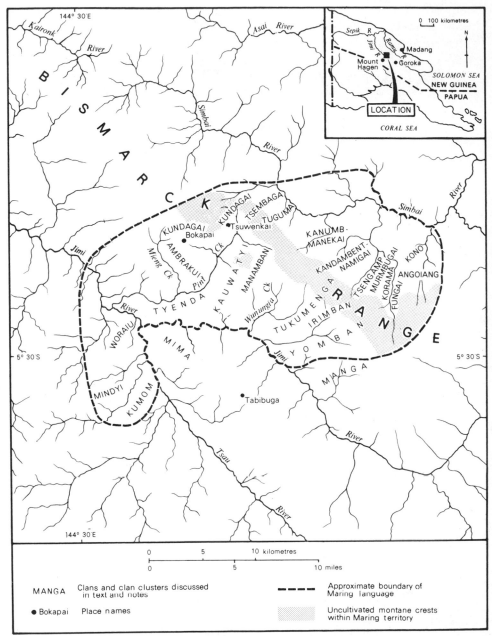

PLATE 1   The Maring Region of New Guinea

Jimi River to the south. About 2,000 of the Marings live in the Simbai Valley and the rest are in the Jimi Valley. People throughout the region engage in traditional subsistence activities: slash-and-burn farming of tuberous staples and other crops, pig husbandry, pandanus tree cultivation, and some gathering of wild plant foods and hunting of feral pigs, small marsupials, and birds.

Population is unevenly distributed, becoming less dense where the Simbai and Jimi Rivers reach lower altitudes—at the eastern end of Maring settlement in the Simbai Valley and the western end in the Jimi Valley. Gross contrasts in density correlate with some differences in the organization of local populations. In the more densely settled areas (which have either close to a hundred people or many more per square mile of land under cultivation or in secondary forest), clan clusters are the largest named groups with recognized territorial boundaries and with members that act together in war and in ceremonies. The core of each of these groups are men who belong to local clans, which are units with members putatively (although often not actually) related through patrilineal descent. Each clan in a cluster is an exogamous unit, but the cluster itself is not. There are about a dozen clusters in the more densely settled Maring areas. If we use the term "clan cluster *population*" to refer to all the people, whether agnates or nonagnates, who live and garden continually on the lands of the clans of a cluster, we can say that the size of clan cluster populations ranges from some 200 to some 850 people.[2]

The same kind of integration of clans into clusters is absent from the less densely settled areas. In warfare here, there were sometimes alliances of clans that had adjacent territories, and it is possible to devise definitions whereby any allied clans may be regarded as constituting a clan cluster.[3] However, it needs to be emphasized that these alliances rarely last for more than a generation, and, even while they are still in force, the allied clans do not necessarily have all friends and enemies in common and they perform separately (and sometimes as hosts and guests rather than as co-hosts) the main ceremonies of the long sequence of rituals which follows warfare.[4] For purposes of the present chapter, it makes sense to refer to allied clans simply as "allied clans" and to reserve the "clan cluster" designation for the more highly integrated, named multiclan groups of the more densely settled Maring areas.

A further contrast between these areas and the lower-density ones lies in the shape and location of group territories. In the former areas, most clusters (and many clans within them) occupy territories that extend in irregular bands from the mossy forests near the crest of the Bismarck Range at an altitude of 6,000 or 7,000 feet to lands at about 2,000 feet at or near the bottom of the Simbai or Jimi valleys.[5] Some clans in the less densely settled areas also have territories dropping from the top of the Bismarck Range, but others have their lands only on small mountains and spurs between either the Simbai or Jimi river and its tributaries and in basins formed by these tributaries.

At the time of our initial anthropological and ecological field work in the Maring region in 1962,[6] the Maring people in general and especially those in the Simbai Valley had experienced hardly any impact yet from missions, trade stores, or labor recruiters. Indeed, although steel axes and bush knives had been introduced along native trade routes in the 1940s, some Maring groups had not been contacted by any white men until four years before our arrival and had not been brought under Australian administrative control until 1960. The last wars between Maring local groups had been fought no more than half a dozen years before our arrival, and the enmities persisting from these wars were still strong among the people in 1962.

The nature of these wars, as reconstructed from informants' accounts, will be indicated in succeeding sections as part of the description of the multiphase process operating among the Marings.

ANTECEDENTS OF FIGHTING

In considering phases of the Maring process, we need not dwell at great length on the peaceful phase immediately preceding the outbreak of fighting. It is possible that a corresponding phase among other peoples—for example, the Maoris (see Chapter 4)—involved increase in the pressure exerted by a group upon its existing territory so that members of the group were stimulated to commit offenses against other groups and were stimulated to commit more and more of them (or increasingly severe ones) as population pressure increased. The provocations to warfare in these cases were cumulative. By contrast, although the provocations to warfare in the Maring case were offenses similar to those characteristic of the prewar phase among the Maoris, the available evidence gives no indication that the offenses had a cumulative effect in provoking war or that their commission correlated with the pressure of particular Maring groups upon their land.

Let us note at this point what the offenses provoking war were. Informants were able to specify the proximate causes of 39 Maring wars for me, and, in almost every case, some offense by the members of one group against the members of another was involved. Murder or attempted murder was the most common offense, having occurred in 22 of the cases. Other offenses mentioned included poaching, theft of crops, and territorial encroachment; sorcery or being accused of sorcery; abducting women or receiving eloped ones; rape; and insults.[7] Sometimes these other offenses led directly to war and sometimes first to homicide and then to war.

It is possible to argue on *a priori* grounds that almost all of these offenses, along with the provocations to commit them, should have increased, among the Marings as among other peoples, with population pressure, which entails a heightening of tensions and of competition over resources. However, it is also possible that the Marings needed less of an accumulation of grievances to incite them to war than did such other peoples as the Maoris. This would be consistent with the fact that among the Marings the account kept of all offenses that one's group made against others and that others made against the group was not as strict as among the Maoris.[8]

More significantly, it would also be consistent with the fact that for each Maring group there were recurrent periods of years when warfare was ritually proscribed. That is to say, if the Marings tended not to undertake wars while the ritual proscriptions were in force, then perhaps they could fight on the basis of fewer provocations than did the Maoris and still not fight so frequently as to jeopardize their survival.[9] The proscriptions became effective after wars and applied to members of the groups that had been the main belligerents and were able to maintain themselves on their own territories. When warfare ended, the men of these groups performed certain rituals. These involved thanking the ancestor spirits for their assistance in the fight, sacrificing for them whatever mature and adolescent pigs were on hand, and promising them many more pigs, truly commensurate with the help received and to be sacrificed when the group had a pig herd large enough for the holding of a festival—something on the order of 170 pigs for a festival hosted by a group of about 200 people.[10]

Until the holding of the festival, warfare was not to be undertaken because, in the Maring view, there would be no help forthcoming from either ancestor spirits or allies until they received their just rewards in pigs. The periods required for raising pig herds considered sufficiently large for a festival thus corresponded as a rule to periods of nonaggression for a group. Moreover, these periods, which lasted usually some ten years, tended to be marked, not only by an absence of open fighting between groups, but also by an absence of provocations or offenses between them. This is because, as will be discussed later, the use of land in places where there was likelihood of contact with members of other groups tended to be avoided by people as long as they could not feel secure in having the support of their ancestor spirits when potentially hostile outsiders or their potentially malefic magic were encountered. In other words, until the ancestor spirits were appeased with pig sacrifices, intergroup offenses were unlikely simply because intergroup encounters were avoided. Obversely, as soon as the outstanding obligations to ancestor spirits and allies had been met, people were more readily disposed to repair to the borderlands of their territories so that encounters with members of other groups and, concomitantly, disputes with them were likely to take place quickly after the conclusion of a pig festival and to lead quickly to warfare. Informants gave accounts of wars that broke out within two or three months or even within weeks after the termination of a group's pig festival.[11]

There is, moreover, no evidence that provocations to war and then warfare itself ensued less quickly after pig festivals among the Maring groups exerting the least pressure upon their land. Some of the smallest Simbai Valley clan populations, living at the edge of a vast expanse of unoccupied forest extending eastward along the

Bismarck Range, fought as often as did some of the large clan cluster populations of the central Maring area, where there are not only higher population densities but also such other indicators of greater pressure upon resources as shorter fallow periods for garden plots, more painstaking harvests from the gardens, and, as a result of more intensive land use in a few places, some tracts of permanent grassland and degraded secondary forest, both of which are rare in the low-density territories.[12] Most Maring groups seem to have averaged one or two wars per generation, and it is in the wars themselves and their aftermaths and not in the antecedents of fighting that we must look for mechanisms operating in response to demographic factors.

TWO PHASES OF WAR: NOTHING FIGHTS AND TRUE FIGHTS

All Maring groups sometimes took part in engagements that they called "small fights" or "nothing fights." In these, the warriors repaired each morning from their homes to prearranged fight grounds at the borders of the lands of the two main belligerent groups. The opposing forces took up positions close enough to each other to be within the range of arrows. Thick wooden shields, as tall as the men and about 2½ feet wide, afforded protection in combat.[13] Sometimes the bottoms of the shields were made to rest on the ground and warriors darted out from behind the shields to shoot their arrows and then darted back. Some men also emerged temporarily from cover in order to taunt their foes and to display their bravery by drawing enemy fire. At the end of each day's fighting, the men returned to their homes. Although these small bow-and-arrow fights sometimes continued for days and even for weeks, deaths or serious injuries in them were rare. Indeed, Rappaport (1967:121–123), in his discussion of the fights as described to him by warriors of the Tsembaga cluster, suggests that, rather than being serious battles, they were, among other things, settings for attempts at conflict resolution by nonviolent means. They brought the antagonists, as he notes, "within the range of each others' voices while keeping them out of the range of each others' deadlier weapons." Sometimes the voices at the fight ground uttered insults, but there also were times

PLATE 2   Maring Warrior, Simbai Valley

when moderation was counseled (especially by men who came as allies of one belligerent group but had ties with the other group as well) and when settlements of disputes were negotiated so as to obviate escalation of the fighting to a more deadly phase.

When there *was* escalation, the Maring pattern was for it to be to a phase involving what informants called "true fights"—fights in which not only bows and arrows and throwing spears but also axes and jabbing spears, the weapons of close combat, were used. While the small fights were still going on, advocates of escalation as well as the Maring equivalents of "doves" were speaking out. Whether the hawks would prevail depended upon a variety of factors—for example, the fighting strength of the enemy as displayed in the "nothing" fight, the casualties, if any, suffered in that fight, and the nature of previous relations between the antagonists. Sometimes a group chose to escalate a fight in order to attempt to even the score with the enemy in killings, while at other times a group abandoned a fight because it had already suffered too many deaths.[14] It is possible that the enemy's show of force in the "nothing" fight was sometimes sufficient to induce a group to flee without submitting to any further test of arms. Accounts that Rappaport (1967:124) received from some Tsembaga informants suggest this. The "nothing" fights may be said to have had what some authors would describe as an epideictic aspect (Rappaport, 1967:195; Wynne-Edwards, 1962:16–17). And, as in the case of other epideictic phenomena, what the fights disclosed to the participants about the size of their rivals' groups could lead to behavior changing the size or dispersion of the groups involved.

If a consensus in favor of escalation to a phase of true fights did develop on both sides, the antagonists, after shouting to each other that the time had come for more serious warfare, withdrew to make elaborate ritual preparations for it for at least two days.[15] When they returned to the fight ground, they took up positions in formations several ranks deep. While men in the opposing front ranks fought duels with one another from behind their huge shields, they were provided with cover by bowmen who were in the ranks further to the rear and who shot at any enemy warriors exposing themselves. Front positions were exchanged for rear ones from time to time in the course of battle, and sometimes individual men temporarily withdrew from combat in order to catch their breath. Most fatalities in these "true" fights seem to have occurred when an enemy arrow or throwing spear brought down a man in the front ranks so that he could be finished off with axes in a quick charge from the enemy's front line. Because of the protection that the shields afforded and because the fighting was from static positions rather than involving any appreciable tactical movements, the warfare could proceed for weeks and even for months without heavy casualties. Each morning when there was to be fighting, the able-bodied men who were the warriors assembled near their hamlets and went *en masse* to the fight ground for their day's combat, while the women remained behind to attend to routine gardening and domestic tasks. The men themselves did not fight daily during the period of warfare. When it rained, both sides stayed in their houses, and, by mutual agreement, all combatants sometimes took a day off to repaint their shields, to attend to rituals in connection with casualties, or simply to rest. There could even be intervals of as long as three weeks during which active hostilities were suspended and the men worked at making new gardens.

It must be emphasized that these truces had to be agreed to by both sides. If only one side absented itself from the fight ground, this was in effect a signal to the other side to consider escalating to another kind of military action: what is to be described below as *routing*. Although this was an action that characteristically lasted but a few hours at the most, it can be usefully discussed as a separate phase in the process of war and peace. Before turning to it, however, we must consider what role allies could have in bringing about routs and what alternative there could be to nothing fights and true fights as the phases of hostilities antecedent to routing.

ALLIES

The prelude to a group's being routed could be a reverse at the fight ground, and this could, as Rappaport (1967:139) has noted in his account of the last war between the Tsembaga and Kundagai clusters in the Simbai Valley, come about through the failure of a

group's allies to appear in force. It should be understood that a
Maring war characteristically had two groups as the main belligerents and that "allies" were men belonging to other groups and
participating in the fighting because of individual ties between them
and the members of the two main belligerent groups. The longer that
fight-ground hostilities dragged on, the more difficult it became for
the main belligerents to maintain the support of allies, who, natu-
rally enough, had their own affairs to attend to. In the case of the
Tsembaga, the greatest number of their allies belonged to the neighboring Tuguma cluster, and it was on the day when the Tuguma did
not come to the fight ground that the Kundagai, still supported by
their own allies and aware of their numerical advantage, mounted a
charge in which the Tsembaga suffered heavy casualties. The routing
of the Tsembaga ensued.

There also were times when a group learned in advance that
needed allies were withdrawing their support. Instead of fighting
and dying in a lost cause, the group would flee to refuge immediately
and its adversaries would be left with only houses and gardens to
destroy but with no people to slaughter in the "routing" phase of
hostilities. The Kanumb group is said to have fled in this manner in
its last war with the Tuguma cluster (Rappaport, 1967:139).

In view of the importance of allies for success in Maring warfare,
it must be understood that whether the support of allies in sufficient
numbers and for long enough time would be forthcoming was not a
capricious matter. Those from whom help might come in warfare
were nonagnatic kinsmen living with other groups and also other
men recruited by such nonagnatic kinsmen. Of the two main belligerent groups in a war, the larger one would thus be likely to have its
numerical advantage magnified by having more allies because,
being larger, it would as a rule have formed more numerous ties with
other groups through marriage. Also, other things being constant,
the group that was doing a better job of using its land and growing
crops and pigs on it would have an advantage for receiving support,
for it would have been more able to make prestations of pigs and
other valuables so as both to maintain the allegiance of existing
kinsmen in other groups and to create new ties through new
marriages.

It needs to be emphasized that merely having kinsmen in other groups was not sufficient to ensure their support. If relations with them had not been kept active through prestations of goods and through services such as helping the kinsmen in their own wars and acting as intermediaries for them in trading goods over long distances, the kinsmen were not likely to be quick to give military assistance. Indeed, a number of Marings that we met had refused to give such assistance to affines whom they felt they had been slighted by. Moreover, it should be noted that the principle of helping kinsmen often left latitude as to where aid should be rendered at a particular time, for one was apt to have different kinsmen engaged in different wars at the same time or even to have them engaged in a single war on opposing sides. Under such circumstances, calculations of self-interest were a factor in decisions about giving aid. Thus, one redoubtable warrior from the Fungai clan initially helped his affines in the Murmbugai clan to fight, but, when he felt himself to have been insufficiently requited for his efforts, he switched to the side of the Murmbugai's enemies, the Korama, a clan that also contained kinsmen of his.

The Kauwatyi cluster of the Jimi Valley, never routed from its territory and with some 850 people in the cluster population, may be cited as an example of a large, aggressive, successful, and centrally located group whose side it was advantageous to be on. The Kauwatyi got even more help than they wanted or needed from their many kinsmen in almost all groups on both sides of the Bismarck Range. According to Kauwatyi informants, the superfluous allies were tolerated at the "nothing" fights and were duly rewarded with pork on subsequent ceremonial occasions but were not asked to join in the more deadly fighting in which any deaths suffered by allies would have had to be recompensed profusely—with brides among the prestations—by the Kauwatyi themselves. No doubt it was an advantage to the Kauwatyi not to have these allies helping the enemy, even if their direct aid on the Kauwatyi side could be dispensed with.

The last war that the Kauwatyi fought was against the Manamban cluster in 1956, and it was a war in which the Kauwatyi did seek allies—but they were allies from a specific group, recruited for a

specific tactical operation. Some of the antecedents and consequences of the involvement of these allies, men from the Tukumenga
cluster, in the war are worth recounting here, for they nicely illustrate the kinds of hardheaded strategic considerations that could be
operative in Maring decisions about launching attacks and becoming
allies. Initially, while the Kauwatyi–Manamban war was going on,
most of the Kauwatyi's Tukumenga allies were involved in hostilities
elsewhere. Tukumenga territory is bordered on the west by the
territory of the Manamban and on the east by the territory of the
Yomban, and one or the other of these clusters has been the enemy in
all but one of the six recent wars in which the Tukumenga have been
one of the main belligerents.[16] At the beginning of 1956 the Tukumenga were not themselves the main belligerents in any war, although large numbers of Tukumenga men were helping the Manga
cluster, a non-Maring group, in fight-ground battle against the
group that had been their own enemy in their last war: the Yomban.[17] Since the Yomban cluster population, with more than 700
people, was about twice the size of the Manga cluster population, the
substantial help received by the Manga from the Tukumenga was no
doubt of critical importance to the Manga cause. When hostilities
broke out between the Kauwatyi and the Tukumenga's other traditional enemy, the Manamban, the war was already on between the
Yomban and the Manga and it was to the Manga that the Tukumenga
men continued to give their help. Each morning they went by a track
near the Jimi River, far from the Yomban settlements, to the
Manga–Yomban fight ground and, after a day of combat, they returned home each evening the same way. This had been going on for
many weeks when, in late April or early May, two of the Kauwatyi
leaders came secretly to the Tukumenga houses (but not to those
where men with Manamban affines might betray the plans) and
asked for the help of the Tukumenga in a concerted attack upon the
Manamban to take place on the following morning. Part of the
proposal was that after defeating and routing the Manamban the
Kauwatyi and Tukumenga would attempt to take over the Manamban territory, with the new boundary between the two victorious
groups to consist of Wunungia Creek in the center of their enemy's
land. The Tukumenga agreed to the plan; the Yomban–Manga war

had been dragging on to no effect, whereas here there was a prospect of a quick and advantageous victory. The Kauwatyi leaders returned to their homes, while the Tukumenga warriors collected their weapons, performed certain prefight rituals,[18] and then made their way to the forests high above their settlements. Here they arranged their shields to form makeshift houses, made fires in the middle of these, and then slept. At dawn they moved along the top of the Bismarck Range and then descended to the Kauwatyi–Manamban fight ground so as to come upon the enemy's rear and take him completely by surprise. The Manamban were easily routed. After joining in the work of destroying the Manamban houses and gardens, the Tukumenga went with the Kauwatyi to the houses of the latter and then returned toward evening to their own houses via the tracks down near the river. On their way back, they could see to the east the smoke and fire which were issuing from the settlements of the Manga: the Yomban had taken advantage of the one-day absence of the Tukumenga. They had mounted a charge which took the lives of five Manga warriors and had followed this up with the routing of the Manga and setting fire to their houses.

AN ALTERNATIVE PHASE: RAIDS

The Tukumenga and Manamban cluster populations each comprised some 600 people, and the size of the Kauwatyi and Yomban populations was, as previously noted, even greater. Only one other Maring group, the Kundagai of the western part of the Maring region in the Jimi Valley, approached these four clusters in size. In the case of the much smaller groups of the less densely settled Maring areas, warfare could be conducted essentially in the manner already described, although, obviously, on a much smaller scale. However, among these groups, another mode of fighting, employed only rarely among the large cluster populations, also seems to have been common and to have constituted an alternative to "nothing fights" and "true fights" as antecedents of routing. This other mode was raiding and consisted usually of stealing in the night to the houses where the men of an enemy clan slept—the 30 or so men in a clan would have their sleeping quarters distributed among perhaps four or five houses. At dawn the raiders would make fast the doors of as many of these houses as possible and then shoot their arrows and poke their long spears through the leaf-thatched walls at the men inside. If the latter succeeded in undoing the doors, they could be picked off by raiders waiting behind the fences of the men's houses for their enemies to emerge. With a numerical advantage on the side of the raiders, these tactics could annihilate the manpower of an enemy clan, which is what may have happened to the Woraiu, a now extinct Maring group that had been living on the south side of the Jimi River where it was attacked by an alliance of the Mindyi and Kumom clans. However, in the accounts that I received from informants in the low-density Maring areas in the eastern Simbai Valley rather than in the Jimi, the raiding force never seems to have been large enough to take care of all enemy men's houses. The raiders in all cases, after killing some men, were forced to retreat because of counterattacks by warriors from houses other than those raided.

These eastern Simbai accounts underscore that this mode of fighting could as a rule be effective only when the enemy group attacked was small. Otherwise, the position of raiders deep in enemy territory could be extremely perilous, for warriors might rise up against them from all sides before they could make good their retreat to their own lands. In light of these considerations, it is not surprising that raiding should have been uncommon among the large cluster populations. Indeed, I was told of only one clear case in which the fighting force of such a population attacked the enemy in his settlements without previously having tested him in fight-ground battle, and it is significant that the attack was made by the Kauwatyi, the largest of the Maring cluster populations, against the Tyenda, a group less than half its size. The Kauwatyi men had gone during the night to Tyenda territory and, at dawn, appeared *en masse* and fully armed at the Tyenda settlements. The Tyenda just ran while the Kauwatyi wrought death and destruction. This attack took place in 1955 and the Kauwatyi suffered no fatalities in it, while the Tyenda, a group of about 300, lost 23 people. It is hardly likely that a similar attack by the Tyenda against the Kauwatyi swarm would have been successful.

ROUTS AND THEIR AFTERMATH

The phase designated here as routing consisted, as already suggested, of going to the enemy settlements, burning the houses there, killing indiscriminately any men, women, or children found in the settlements, and, after having put the survivors to flight, destroying gardens, fences, and pandanus groves, and defiling the burial places. These proceedings sometimes took place immediately after the enemy warriors had broken ranks and fled in response to a charge at the fight ground. That is to say, the fleeing warriors would rush to their hamlets, gather their women and children, and then flee on to seek refuge, while the routers wreaked as much death and destruction as they could. This is what happened in the war in which the Kauwatyi and Tukumenga jointly routed the Manamban. At other times, the routing did not take place until the day after losses at the fight ground; the side that had suffered them would fail to appear and its antagonists would thereupon proceed to the settlements to burn and to kill. A Yomban-Tukumenga fight had this outcome.

Routing was not an inevitable consequence of the "true" wars of the Marings. It was possible, before events moved into the routing phase, for both sides to opt for an armistice whereby there could be no warfare between them until the holding of massive pig festivals such as were referred to earlier. Rappaport (1967:143) has suggested that armistice was the more likely course when the number of killings between the antagonists was equal or when both agreed that, regardless of any disparities in the homicide score, the pressure of subsistence tasks made it impractical to continue hostilities. This may well be. However, on the basis of information about warfare involving either the Tsembaga or Tuguma cluster, Rappaport (1967:142) has made the further suggestion that "true" wars of the Marings ended most frequently with armistice. This suggestion is not in accord with the accounts that informants gave me concerning the termination of 29 such wars. Nineteen of these ended with the routing of people and the destruction of their homes and gardens. The important point is that the phase of "true" wars, like that of "nothing" fights, was one from which there could be either a return to peace or else escalation to a phase leading to further testing of the antagonists. That this was testing, not only of the belligerents' capacity to defend themselves, but also of their capacity to defend and use their land can be seen in the aftermath of routs.

The routs themselves did not necessarily have a decisive effect on these capacities. The Woraiu, as noted in the preceding section, may have had their manpower effectively destroyed when they were raided by the Mindyi and Kumom, but such annihilation of the fighting force of a group cannot have been common in Maring warfare. The Marings, unlike such other peoples as the Maoris, did not customarily pursue an enemy beyond his settlements. To have done so would have been, according to informants, inviting one's own death and so, as already indicated, the victors stayed behind and burned houses, ravaged gardens, and performed other destructive acts. The two Maring wars in which informants belonging to defeated groups claimed to have suffered the heaviest losses were the ones fought against the Kauwatyi by the Tyenda and the Manamban in the mid-1950s. When some 300 Tyenda were routed following the Kauwatyi's surprise raid, 14 Tyenda men, 6 women, and 3 children were killed. The Manamban, with a population of some 600, lost only 8 men and 3 women in the course of being routed by the combined forces of the Kauwatyi and Tukumenga (although there had been 20 other Manamban deaths at the fight ground previously). If these figures indicate the heaviest mortality suffered in Maring wars, it may be questioned whether routs in general were effective in decisively altering the capacity of groups to defend and use their land.

Let us consider then the testing of the antagonists in the aftermath of routs—first of all, during the period or phase which may be described as that of refuging by the routed group. The first opportunity that such a group had to show its mettle in this period was in the selection of a place of refuge. I have accounts of 21 routs. In 7 of these, the routed groups did not even leave their own territory but rather took refuge in portions of it at some distance from the borderlands where their enemies had engaged them. Among the routed groups in the 14 other cases, there were some whose members fled across the Bismarck Range or the major rivers for refuge but there were others whose members remained closer to their own territories and, indeed, sometimes continued to maintain a claim to these by going to portions of them for food from their residences on the lands of friendly neighbors.

In the case of groups taking refuge outside of their own territories, a major test versus the enemies that had routed them lay in making the return to their own lands. Rappaport's discussion of routs suggests that defeated groups often failed to do this (Rappaport, 1967:145). However, in 13 of my 14 cases, the routed groups did indeed return; the one exception involved the Woraiu, who, as noted earlier, may have had their manpower effectively destroyed when they were raided by the Mindyi and Kumom. Unfortunately, the interpretation of these data is made difficult by the fact that the routed groups, in 7 of the cases referred to, made their returns after the Australian administration had established its presence in the Maring region. It may be—as, indeed, Rappaport (1967:145) has suggested it was—that some of the groups, especially after having fragmented for the sake of obtaining refuge in one or another of the places where there were kinsmen or friends of individuals in the groups, would not have reconstituted themselves and repossessed their territories if not for the security and protection that the Australian presence afforded. There is, unfortunately, no evidence on which firm conclusions about this may be based. It seems likely, however, that Australian intervention did enable some groups to return to their territories more quickly and to rebuild their settlements in closer proximity to those of their enemies than would have been the case otherwise. This was most notably so in the case of the Manga. After being routed by the Yomban in 1956, they fled across the Jimi for refuge with friends and kinsmen living around a place called Tabibuga. From there, word of the Manga defeat was carried south across the Wahgi–Sepik Divide to Minj, the Australian government's subdistrict headquarters for the Western Highlands District in New Guinea. The Assistant District Officer there had visited the Yomban–Manga area previously with armed patrols—in 1953 and 1955. When an aerial survey confirmed the destruction of the Manga settlements, a new patrol was organized and it marched along the tracks to the area some time in May, less than a month after the routing of the Manga. The Manga themselves were first taken back to their land by the patrol, which then proceeded to move against the

Yomban. The ambushes that Yomban warriors armed with axes had prepared for the patrol were unsuccessful, but the Yomban neverthe-less continued to shower arrows upon the patrol and finally fled only after six of their number had been shot dead by New Guinea police-men armed with rifles. This intervention, however, was quickly followed by one that was to have a more continuous impact upon war and peace among the Marings of the Jimi Valley: the establish-ment of a Patrol Post at Tabibuga, with an Australian Officer-in-Charge and a complement of rifle-armed native policemen to extend *Pax Australiensis* into the Jimi Valley. Tabibuga is but a couple of hours' walk from the Manga settlements, and so, with the establish-ment of the Patrol Post, the Manga had the security to devote themselves to rebuilding their houses on their former sites and to using their lands once more.[19]

Members of some other groups, perhaps partly because of the greater distance of their territories from Tabibuga, were more hesi-tant about leaving their refuges, but eventually all of the Jimi Valley groups, with varying degrees of help and supervision from Tabi-buga, were repatriated. From July through October of 1956 there were monthly visits to the "disturbed" Maring areas of the Jimi Valley either by the Tabibuga officer or by other Australian officials. Among the instructions given to the people on the occasion of the visits were that they were to rebuild their houses and gardens, to report any raids to the Tabibuga Patrol Officer, and to "keep their own noses clean" unless they wished to be "very severely dealt with." Weapons also were collected and burned publicly. By early October the Tabibuga officer, Barry Griffin, was able to make the statement that all of the recently routed Maring-speaking groups of the Jimi Valley—the Ambrakui, the Manamban, and the Tyenda—had, like the Narak-speaking Manga, been restored to their lands.

Actually, the statement, at least in October 1956, could not be made accurately without qualifications, and the qualifications called for are suggestive as to what might have been the aftermath of the routs in the absence of government intervention. While all of the groups had been restored to some degree, there were, it must be noted, variations in the degree. Thus, the Ambrakui, who had been routed some time around 1954 as a result of fighting that began with land encroachments by the Kundagai,[20] had taken refuge on the south side of the Jimi River, mainly on the lands of the Mima cluster, which included numerous affines and friends of the Ambrakui. From Mima territory, some of the Ambrakui accompanied a patrol led by Griffin at the end of September 1956 to their abandoned territory north of the river. Griffin instructed them to resettle there and left a few policemen in the general area to help in the work. He also held discussions with both Kundagai and Ambrakui about their lands and then affirmed boundaries which, according to what I was told by Ambrakui informants in 1963, corresponded to the ancestral ones between the lands of the two groups. However, when Griffin revisited the Ambrakui territory in June of 1957 he saw that the resettlement of the people, averred by him in October of the previous year, was still far from complete: the men had, in effect, simply been visiting their old lands, while the women, children, and pigs had, for the most part, not even been doing that; they had been remaining in their Mima refuges. And new gardens had not been made in the old lands. Only with increased police supervision and with further warnings to the Kundagai was the full return of the Ambrakui to their territory finally effected later in 1957. Less than five years later there were new land encroachments by the Kundagai. In response to the complaints of the Ambrakui about this, the Tabibuga Patrol Officer (a successor of Griffin) sent policemen to destroy Kundagai plantings on Ambrakui land and to arrest the offending Kundagai and bring them to jail in Tabibuga. These incidents show that the Ambrakui, having only some 250 people in the cluster population and thus one of the smallest of the Maring clusters in the Jimi Valley, still had in the Kundagai a powerful enemy that was ready to act aggressively unless stopped by superior force. Any Ambrakui skittishness about being repatriated is perhaps not surprising.

In contrast to this, members of the large and powerful Manamban cluster, after having fled for refuge to at least ten different groups on both sides of the Bismarck Range, began drifting back to their own territory within a week or two of having been routed by the Kauwatyi and Tukumenga in late April or early May of 1956. When the patrol from the subdistrict headquarters at Minj arrived to confront the Yomban, some Manamban were already back on their land

and a delegation of them went to Yomban territory to meet with the Australian officer. A government patrol that included Manamban territory in its itinerary in July 1956 reported that the Manambans had not yet returned from their routing but that a fair gathering of them nevertheless assembled. According to the head count made, there were 239 people. This constitutes about 40% of the Manamban cluster population. When Griffin arrived 16 days later to make a census, he saw 305 people and recorded their names. The return of the remaining people proceeded smoothly thereafter.

The third routed people, the Tyenda, seemed to have been intermediate in their readiness to be repatriated—less timid than the Ambrakui, less bold than the Manamban. Not a large group, they nevertheless had had support even in refuge from numerous allies among the powerful Kundagai and Manamban. The former was the group that most of the Tyenda had been refuging with following their rout at the hands of the Kauwatyi in 1955, and they had continued to go to their own lands for food while in refuge. Indeed, on one occasion, they had killed four Kauwatyi men pursuing a pig deep into Tyenda territory and the Kauwatyi were thereafter afraid to go far beyond the old boundary between the lands of the two groups. As for the Manambans, their support for the Tyenda in refuge had been demonstrated by their response to a Tyenda kinsman's pleas for revenge against the Kauwatyi who had killed his children and brothers; the Manamban had gone *en masse* to challenge their old enemies by killing a Kauwatyi man. This was the killing that had led to the Kauwatyi–Manamban war ending with the rout of the Manamban in 1956. The enmity between the Kauwatyi and the Manamban had of course been of long standing, but this very fact points up a difference between the position of the Tyenda and that of the Ambrakui, for the latter had no strong group to which they could turn to make common cause against the powerful enemy that had routed them. It is consistent with this that when the Ambrakui were still remaining close to their Mima refuges in June 1957 the Tyenda were found by Griffin to be going ahead well with resettlement and to have prepared extensive new gardens in their own territories. On the basis of the variations in the tempo of resettlement even with government support, it may be supposed that in the absence of such support the

Ambrakui would not have returned to their land but the Manamban would have and so, perhaps, at least to part of their land, would have the Tyenda.

Groups failing to return to their territories would, in effect, be leaving them for other groups eventually to annex, and such annexation is what marks off the final phase of the war process. But what happened to groups and their lands after warfare in which no group had been permanently routed from its entire territory? This is the question with which we must now deal.

TWO KINDS OF PEACE: WITH AND WITHOUT LAND REDISTRIBUTION

Usually the defeated groups, whether they had been routed from their territory or not, made new settlements further than their old ones from their borders with the enemies that had beaten them. In the Maring view, the rationale for this course of action was not only to avoid the enemies but also to avoid their malefic magic, thought by the Marings to infest the borderlands where the fighting had taken place. The worse the defeat had been, the more the enemy and his magic were to be feared, and, in extreme cases, new settlements of a group were made deep within the forests that had previously been used by the group for hunting rather than for gardens or long-term residences.[21] At times, the new settlements were made not even in the group's own territory, although that continued to be used by the group for making gardens and for other economic activities. Houses, however, were constructed on the land of a neighboring group that was friendly. This constitutes in effect the same pattern of settlement and land use as operated among the Tyenda while they were refuging with the Kundagai but continuing to use their own lands. The pattern is noted here again because it was put into effect by some groups like the Tsembaga (see Rappaport, 1967:145) and the Murmbugai of the Simbai Valley, not when in their original places of refuge after having been routed, but rather when they had returned from those places to use their own territories (even if not to live on them) once more. The Murmbugai were still following this pattern in

1963, some seven or eight years after they had been defeated by the Kandambent–Namigai group. And this was not the first time that the Murmbugai had done this. The Korama clan had destroyed their houses in an earlier war and they had made new ones on the Tsengamp clan's territory, whence they issued forth in due time to destroy the Korama settlements.

Some defeated groups succeeded in rehabilitating themselves fully. The gardens that they made on their lands grew well, their pig herds increased, their allies stood by them, and they accumulated the wherewithal to make the appropriate sacrifices to appease the ancestor spirits. The members of such groups eventually felt strong enough and secure enough to stand up to their old enemies and their magic and, some 10 years after the warfare, they would return to the borderlands, utter spells there to chase the enemy spirits and the corruption caused by them back to enemy territory, and then plant new boundary stakes where the old ones had been before the fighting.[22] This last action signified that the *status quo ante bellum* was to be restored as far as territories were concerned—that there was to be peace without land redistribution. The stake-planting would be followed by a pig festival in which, as previously noted, the outstanding obligations to allies and ancestor spirits would be met and their help in future encounters with enemies would thus, most beneficially for the group's morale, be secured.

But not all defeated groups that gained their subsistence from their own lands after warfare had their confidence—and the grounds for confidence—restored to this same high degree. For some groups, perhaps with the loss of men and destruction of resources suffered in warfare compounded by post-bellum adversities such as diseases affecting themselves or their pigs, the borderlands where the enemy, his spirits, and his magic were thought to lurk continued to be places of fearsome peril. If a group did not rehabilitate itself sufficiently to be able to assert itself at its old boundaries by planting stakes there, it might simply leave some of its territory to be annexed by its enemies. An example of this is discussed by Rappaport (1967:171): part of the land from which the Tsembaga had driven their enemies was not reclaimed and was accordingly annexed to Tsembaga territory. My own informants were unable to cite any examples from recent Maring wars, but they did refer to certain dispositions by the Tyenda as an example of an alternative that groups not strong enough to confront their old enemies at the borderlands might have recourse to. The dispositions occurred after the last defeat of the Tyenda at the hands of the Kauwatyi and consisted of giving to the Kundagai groups of Bokapai and Tsuwenkai about 1.8 square miles of land in the higher altitudes in the northern part of Tyenda territory. This land, running as a band from the crest of the Bismarck Range down to the Pint River and, in its lower reaches which are best suited for gardens, bordering Kundagai territory on the west and Kauwatyi territory on the east, comprised about 30–40% of the total territory of the Tyenda. By giving the land to their Kundagai friends (including those who had provided them with refuge after their rout by the Kauwatyi), the Tyenda were requiting the Kundagai for their help in the past, making future help from them more likely, and, perhaps most importantly, arranging to have friends rather than enemies at the boundary between the land that the Tyenda were relinquishing and the land to which they were holding on. It must be added that in this last regard the Tyenda were not completely successful, for the Kauwatyi quickly appropriated for their own agricultural use some of the ground in question, that is to say, before the Kundagai had a chance to occupy it. As af result, the Kundagai, kept by the *Pax Australiensis* from seeking redress through the traditional recourse to arms, were planning to bring the Kauwatyi before the government courts over the matter. These effects can be argued also to have been advantageous for the Tyenda—insofar as they were diverting the hostility and aggressions of the Kauwatyi from the Tyenda themselves to the Kundagai. In any event, a more densely settled group—whether the Kundagai or the Kauwatyi—was getting land from the Tyenda, a group with relatively low population density before its bestowal of its northern territory upon the Kundagai.[23] The example suggests that there may have been a variety of ways in which land redistribution following routing and refuging took place and that some of these ways may themselves have been multiphase processes. The fact that in our exposition here we have distinguished, not multiple post-refuging phases involving land redistribution, but rather only a single phase designated as "peace with land redistribution" (see Plate 3) may well constitute an oversimplifica-

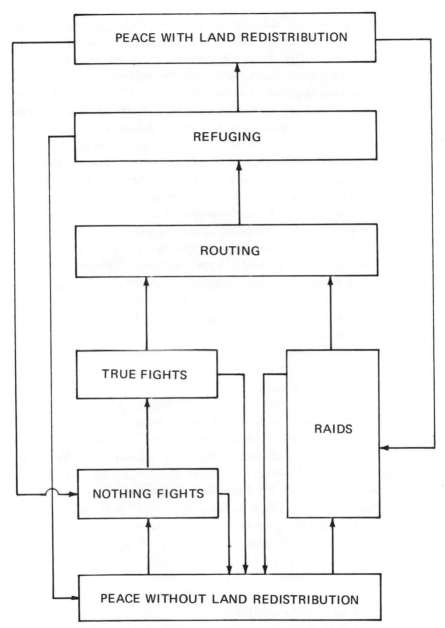

PLATE 3 The Process of War among the Marings

tion of processes that actually took place in the Maring past. If, however, this should be the case, it must be said that the oversimplification is unavoidable, since the post-refuging land-redistribution processes have hardly been operating recently and details about them are, accordingly, hard to come by.

By regarding peace without land redistribution and peace with it as *alternative* phases antecedent to new rounds of fighting, we may be guilty of further oversimplification. Some hazy accounts of events that took place long ago suggest that land redistribution could be a slow post-bellum process involving groups that had appeared initially not to have relinquished any of their lands. An example of such an account concerns an originally autonomous group—either clan or clan cluster—called the Kombepe. Towards the end of the last century, before any of our informants had been born, the Kombepe people had their own discrete territory in the low altitudes between the Mieng and Pint creeks and were neighbors of both the Kundagai and the Ambrakui and had a number of affines in each of these groups. When a dispute arose between some Kundagai and Kombepe, the Kundagai took their affines among the Kombepe to the Kundagai settlements for safety and then made an attack upon the remaining Kombepe. Of these, the ones surviving the attack went as a group to live with the Ambrakui and now constitute a clan of the Ambrakui cluster. In other words, the Kombepe split into two separate groups and ceased to exist as a single autonomous group. They did not, however, thereby cease to maintain their rights to their ancestral ground. Some of this continued as the land of the Kombepe staying with the Kundagai and the rest of it as the land of the Kombepe affiliated with the Ambrakui. But the two groups of Kombepe made grants of usufruct to their respective hosts. In the case of the Kundagai Kombepe, their failure to have many descendants resulted in the eventual complete absorption of themselves and their lands by the Kundagai.

SUMMARY AND DISCUSSION

Some features of the Maring multiphase process are especially important for understanding how war processes can operate adaptively in relation to perturbations that people must deal with. These features are noted below.

1. *The later phases of the process which involve heavy mortality and lead sometimes to territorial conquests cannot occur unless preceded by periods of weeks or months marked by rather ritualized hostilities in which mortality is low.* In many Maring wars, the first phase of these hostilities consisted of a succession of "nothing fights," which were day-long bow-and-arrow encounters at a prearranged battleground. This phase could continue for many days and even weeks. The succeeding phase consisted of "true fights," in which the arms employed at the battleground were expanded to include weapons of close combat and the warriors sometimes made quick charges into the enemy lines. However, in most of the fighting of this phase, the combatants remained in static positions behind large shields and, accordingly, engagements could take place day after day for weeks and even months without heavy casualties. Moreover, hostilities could, by mutual agreement, be suspended for a day or more during this phase in order to allow the combatants to repaint their shields, to attend to rituals in connection with casualties, to rest, or to attend to agricultural tasks. Mortality became heavy, as a rule, only when there was escalation to a phase which can be called routing. In this, the warriors of one side went to the enemy settlements, burned the houses there, killed indiscriminately any men, women, or children that they found, and, after having put the survivors to flight, destroyed gardens, fences, and pandanus groves, and defiled the burial places.

2. *Escalations from phase to phase in the war process are not inevitable: what was referred to in the first chapter as an "inescapable playing-out of forces set in motion at the outset" does not obtain.* A return to peace is possible from each of a number of the phases of war: from "nothing fights," from "true fights," and from the phase of raids which, especially in the low-density parts of the Maring area, is an alternative to "nothing fights" and "true fights" as antecedents to routing. Decisions by both sides in favor of armistice were influenced by assessments of relative fighting strength, numbers of casualties, and the nature of previous relations between the antagonists. Moreover, from the refuging that followed routing, there also could be a return to the *status quo ante bellum.* It might be expected

PLATE 4   Repainting a War Shield, Jimi Valley

that the land of a routed group whose members had gone into refuge would have been immediately taken by the victorious warriors. The latter, however, were constrained by Maring notions about the continuing dangerousness of the ancestor spirits of displaced enemies and, accordingly, would not attempt to move into the enemy land until a later time—perhaps many years later—when they could count on the support of their own ancestor spirits because of having made appropriate sacrifices of pigs to them in a long sequence of ceremonies. If, however, the routed group succeeded in rehabilitating itself and returning to its old lands before any move by the victorious warriors, no territorial annexations would take place.

3. *The causes of entry into war are not the same as the causes of escalation from one phase to another of the war process.* The Maring data show that wars which begin for revenge for murders or other offenses committed against the group—and these were almost always what led Maring men to war—can end with territorial conquests. Similar evidence could be cited from the Maori case study in Chapter 4. Such evidence raises, as some scholars have recognized (e.g., Naroll and Divale, n.d.), serious questions about the validity of cross-cultural or cross-societal studies which depend on the fixed assignment of the warfare of various societies to one or another of a limited number of such categories as "revenge warfare" (e.g., Numelin, 1950:105; Wright, 1965:373). Our evidence points to the possibility that the ethnographic reports on which the assignments to the categories are based may be describing the causes of only the first phases of war processes in which fighting for blood revenge or magical trophies or sacrificial victims can become something else if there is escalation to the later phases.

4. *Perturbations can be counteracted when there is escalation to the final phase of the war process.* The fighting in the early phases of the Maring war process and also, if there was escalation, in the later ones tested for disparities among neighboring groups in such variables as military strength. The fighting thus enabled groups suffering from population pressure to discover at whose (if anybody's) expense territorial expansion, providing relief from the pressure, might take place. In other words, relief could be achieved if there were escalation to territorial conquests after a due period of testing for dispari-

ties in such variables as military strength. (The requirement of this
period of testing and the fact that the war process was a multiphase
one allowed time for recourse to nonwarlike means for seeking relief
from stresses associated with population pressure; these means,
described in other publications on the Marings [e.g., Rappaport,
1969], included various kinds of peaceful land transfers between
individuals and between groups and also peaceful shifts of residence.)

Examples of aggressive Maring groups that were suffering from
population pressure (as will be discussed shortly) and sought relief
from it through warfare are the Kauwatyi and Kundagai. They probably would have found relief by means of escalation to territorial
conquests in the final phase of the war process if the Australian
administration had not intervened.[24]

5. *The war process may persist even if the conditions conducive to
escalation to territorial conquests are absent for long periods; such persistence is not necessarily nonadaptive.* Maring warfare in recent times
often ended without escalation to territorial conquests. Why was this
so? The question is one that we must deal with in order to see more
clearly how the war process may persist while the conditions conducive to escalation to territorial conquests are absent.

A possible answer is that population decline has left most Maring groups with numbers which, on the one hand, could be sustained adequately from each group's existing lands and which, on
the other hand, were insufficient for effective exploitation of additional lands. Although detailed demographic and ecological data for
substantiation of this possibility are lacking, various observations in
accord with it may be made. Thus, we do have evidence that, at the
time of our field work, Maring population as a whole had been
declining for some years, apparently mainly because many Marings
had not yet developed resistance to diseases introduced with the
advent of Europeans. A dysentery epidemic carried off at least
20% of the population of some groups in the late 1930s or early
1940s, and, in more recent years, the average rate of population
decline for Maring groups has been almost 1% per year. This is a
preliminary estimate from census data analyzed by Buchbinder
(1973).

There can, of course, have been population decline without its having been of such magnitude and generality as to have eliminated any appreciable pressure to which the territories of particular groups may have previously been subjected. The fact is, however, that when we were doing our field work in the 1960s we could find no clear evidence of such pressure anywhere in the Maring region except in Kauwatyi and Kundagai territory, where there were extensive tracts of permanent grassland and degraded secondary forest. Apart from this, the indicators of pressure and concomitant environmental deterioration such as are to be found in more intensively exploited parts of the New Guinea highlands were absent—no sediment-laden streams and no rill wash or sheet erosion except on trails, bare clay houseyards, and occasional landslides (compare Street, 1969:105 on the Chimbu region, with Street, n.d.:4–5 on the Maring region).

An absence of pressure on the territories of most Maring groups is suggested also by the amount of their land which is primary forest ("PF" for short).[25] Aerial photographs of the territories of Maring groups containing 3,240 people, almost half of the total Maring population, are available (see Note 2); these territories constitute an area of 55 square miles and 40% of it is in PF. Overall population density per square mile of PF in this area is 150, and only one group, with 800 people per square mile of such forest, seems to have less forest than it needs. No other groups have more than 245 people per square mile of PF. The groups with ample PF could subsist from new gardens made in some of it when they were compelled by warfare or other circumstances to abandon their garden sites and settlements in secondary forest tracts.[26]

Significantly, the group with the proportionately least amount of PF is the Kauwatyi. According to informants from the group, the Kauwatyi have imposed upon themselves a taboo whereby no gardens may be made in the little more than a square mile which they have in PF. It must be noted that such forest is an important resource area in its own right—a source of game, firewood, building materials, and various wild food plants.[27] The Kauwatyi, like other Maring groups, had to keep some land in PF in order to have access to these resources. The unavailability of Kauwatyi land for what might be called "internal pioneering"—a group's conversion of PF within its own territories into garden land—may have been an important factor promoting the land encroachments and aggressions by the Kauwatyi against other groups.[28] Only one group besides the Kauwatyi committed land encroachments that led to warfare in recent times. This group was the Kundagai of Bokapai, who, in the mid-1950s, fought the Ambrakui after having begun to make gardens on Ambrakui land. The Kundagai are not among the groups whose land in PF can be estimated from the available aerial photographs, but Kundagai informants did tell me that their group was short of such land. It is noteworthy that the Kundagai and Kauwatyi are the two large Maring groups which, as suggested earlier, might have succeeded in permanently displacing other groups and taking over all or part of their territory if not for the intervention of the Australian administration.

But what is important in the context of answering the question about nonescalation to territorial conquests is not so much the indications of pressure for the Kauwatyi and the Kundagai but rather the absence of clear indications for the other groups. Does this mean, however, that these other groups were not suffering at all from pressure which might have been conducive to territorial conquests on their part? The answer here must be that it does not necessarily mean this, for, as I myself have argued elsewhere (Vayda, 1961a:353–354), it is unjustified to assume that a group will take land from its neighbors only when the source of pressure is its having numbers as great as or possibly even greater than the numbers that its existing territory can continue to support under a given system of land use. Food supplies diminishing slowly as the size of a group increases might, for example, predispose members of the group to territorial conquests long before they attain numbers equivalent to the maximum which their original territory can carry and long before there is readily visible environmental deterioration (cf. Birdsell, 1957:54). Unfortunately we do not have the data that might indicate how far such a process of diminution of food supplies had gone (if it was operating at all) among particular Maring groups at particular times. And while Rappaport (1967:87–96 and Appendix 10) has made some calculations of the carrying capacity of Tsembaga territory and has tentatively concluded that Tsembaga numbers were well below capacity, we have no adequate basis for making reliable estimates of just how much below the carrying capacities of their territories were the sizes of various groups at different times and in different parts of the Maring region. Such estimates would have to be based on ecological investigations more lengthy and comprehensive than those which have been made throughout the Maring region or throughout any other region where there has been primitive warfare in recent times (see Street, 1969). In short, we cannot claim categorically that absence of population pressure among Marings other than the Kauwatyi and Kundagai explains the nonescalation to territorial conquests in recent Maring warfare.

Nevertheless, even if there were significant pressure of which we are not aware in the Maring region, it is clear enough that there was nothing comparable in magnitude to the pressure associated with territorial conquests among such people of the New Guinea highlands as the Central Enga, whose region is much more densely settled and intensively exploited than is the Maring region.[29] As noted by Meggitt (1957a:135–136; 1965:82, 218; 1972:118–120), when population increase was adding to the pressure on the resources of centrally located Enga clans, there was no unoccupied arable land for their extra members to use and the conquests of the territories of other clans were attempted. Enga warfare regularly featured the destruction of weaker clans and resulted in a continual redistribution of arable land between groups.

Such contrasts to the Maring situation make it reasonable to hypothesize that there are certain thresholds of pressure that groups such as those of the Maring and Enga regions must reach before they will undertake territorial conquests and, further, that Enga and other highland groups[30] were attaining these thresholds in recent times while Maring groups, with the exception of the Kauwatyi and Kundagai, were not. In the absence of more precise quantitative data, we can regard this only as a working hypothesis—which, it would be hoped, would lead to further field investigations. However, it is appropriate to consider here now a matter to which the hypothesis relates: the persistence of processes like the Maring war process.

Much of recent Maring warfare as I have described it here and early nineteenth century Maori warfare as described in Chapter 4 were similar in having features that could be interpreted as no longer doing something they had formerly done, i.e., as no longer leading to territorial conquests as a means of obtaining relief from population pressure. Does this mean that the persistence of war processes among the Maoris and Marings should be characterized as maladaptive? The answer to this question with respect to the Maoris is discussed in Chapter 4. With respect to the Marings, the answer is no. Unlike fighting for revenge among the Maoris after the spread of muskets throughout New Zealand, recent Maring warfare was operating in a manner both appropriate to the prevailing demographic and ecological conditions and in keeping with the traditional functioning of the system of response processes in which Maring fighting, routing, refuging, and returning from refuge were components. In other words, as suggested by the hypothesis just discussed, even if territorial conquests had been only a very infrequent rather than a regular aftermath of Maring warfare for a considerable time, the warfare remained the kind that could, through an already institutionalized systemic process, lead again to population dispersion and land redistribution whenever demographic and ecological conditions changed sufficiently to make it appropriate for this to happen. That the persistence of the process should not be regarded as maladaptive or even merely nonadaptive is further indicated by the fact that significant change in demographic and ecological conditions was a continuing possibility in the Maring region: new crops or new diseases could be introduced; the size of a population could be swelled by the arrival of refugees from elsewhere (cf. Watson, 1970); the demography of particular local groups could be drastically altered as, in the course of shifting their garden sites and residences in accordance with the requirements of shifting cultivation, they unwittingly moved either into a malarial zone or out of it. In other words, the war process was likely to be needed again as an adaptive response to stresses associated with population pressure.[31]

3

IBAN HEADHUNTING
A Persistent Process

Turning from New Guinea, the world's second largest island (after Greenland), to Borneo, the third largest, allows us to continue the analysis of multiphase processes responding to perturbations and involving warfare of various modes and intensities. In the preceding chapter, an exploration was begun of the persistence of such processes. Here the exploration is continued by means of an examination of headhunting among the Iban people of Sarawak, with special reference to the question of how the processes are affected when the arena within which they occur is enlarged. We will be looking at headhunting as practiced near and far by the Ibans.

BORNEO, SARAWAK, THE WHITE RAJAHS, AND THE IBANS

Numbering more than 200,000, the Ibans are at present the largest indigenous ethnic group in the Malaysian State of Sarawak, which is one of the three small states into which Borneo's northern

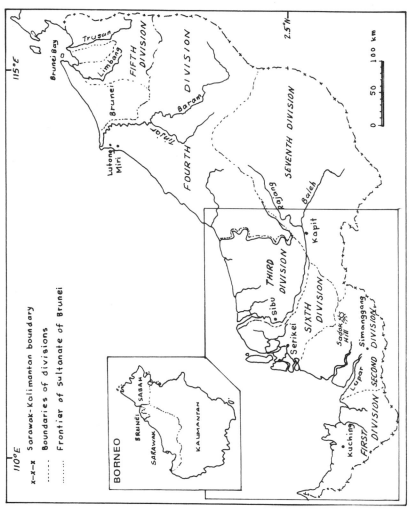

PLATE 5   Borneo and Sarawak: Boundaries and Frontiers

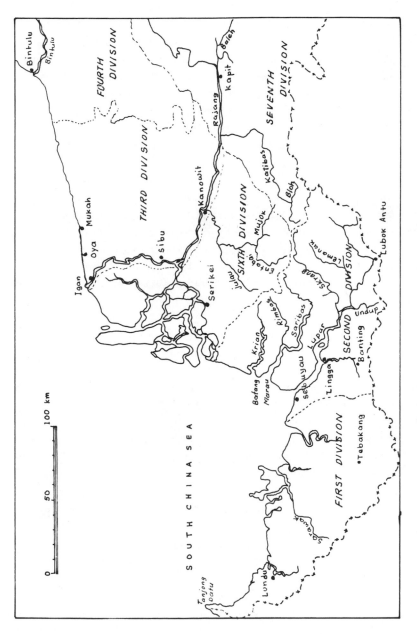

PLATE 6   Southwest Sarawak

and northwestern part, comprising about 30% of the 293,000 square miles of the island, is divided. The other two states are Brunei and the Malaysian State of Sabah. The remainder of the island is Indonesian (formerly Dutch) Borneo or Kalimantan. Sarawak, with which we will be primarily concerned, now has an area of 48,250 square miles (about the same as England), but it was considerably smaller in 1841 when an Englishman, James Brooke, was beginning to establish his government there. Brooke, inspired by Sir Stamford Raffles's vision of British dominion in the Eastern Seas, first visited Sarawak in 1839 in a small armed schooner bought with part of an inheritance that he had recently received. The following year, he provided decisive help to nobles from Brunei (which had nominal suzerainty in Sarawak) in battle against a coalition of local Malay chiefs and their pagan allies. In return for this help, Brooke obtained as his personal domain an area roughly equivalent to Sarawak's present First Division. British naval support during the 1840s enabled him to consolidate his position as the white rajah of Sarawak, but Britain refused to assume any responsibility for ruling there during Brooke's lifetime. When he died in 1868 and his nephew, Charles Brooke, became the second white rajah, Sarawak included the present Second, Third, Sixth, and Seventh Divisions and also part of the Fourth Division (see Plates 5 and 6) and was still independent. There will be references to the white rajahs throughout the pages to follow, although our main focus will be on the Ibans in pre-Brooke times and in only the first years of Brooke rule.

Modern Ibans are sometimes regarded as still belonging to a number of different tribes, but, with headhunting no longer practiced, the boundaries between these have become blurred. Formerly, a tribe among the Ibans was a group whose members did not take one another's heads—a loose, largely endogamous territorial group composed of kindreds that were related (albeit sometimes remotely) and were dispersed in longhouse communities along the banks of a major river and its tributaries (Freeman, 1970:126–127). Ibans cultivate what they call swamp rice in some downriver areas (Pringle, 1970:26), but their main subsistence activity in Sarawak's interior is—and has long been—the growing of dry rice on impermanent hillside clearings in the tropical rainforest, an activity well described

PLATE 7 Iban Longhouse, Third Division

in J. D. Freeman's classic monograph, *Iban Agriculture* (1955). The shifting cultivation of hill rice is one of two practices to which the Ibans have been noted to have an unusually intense devotion (Pringle, 1970:21). The other is headhunting, to be scrutinized in the following pages.

HEADHUNTING NEAR

In the years during which the Ibans were acquiring their reputation as the "most inveterate head-hunters" of Borneo (Hose and McDougall, 1912:I, 187) and even "the wickedest head-hunters . . . perhaps in the whole world" (MacDonald, 1956:10), various motives, some of which will be discussed later, were attributed to the people to account for their commitment to taking heads. However, one basic motive is particularly important for understanding how headhunting might have worked as part of a process responding to stresses associated with population pressure. This motive was formerly widespread among headhunting peoples of both insular and mainland Southeast Asia (see Fürer-Haimendorf, 1967:100; 1969:95; Hutton, 1921:160 ff.; 1928; 1930; McCarthy, 1959:76; Mills, 1926a:200; 1926b; 1935; 1937:61), and is well described in the following passage by Kennedy, who regards other motives as superficial and finds the basic reasons for Indonesian headhunting to lie in people's ideas about the magical power of human heads:

> A Borneo settlement, let us say, has been suffering from epidemics, crop failures, and infertility of women. Casting about for a reason to explain their ill-fortune, they arrive at the characteristically Indonesian notion that their group lacks magical power. Their spiritual "juice" is running low. What they need is a fresh influx of supernatural vigor, not only to strengthen themselves, their crops and their women, but also to fight off evil spirits with greater effectiveness.
> One of the most direct means of getting the magical power they need is to capture a new batch of heads from some other group. The spiritual energy of the other settlement is most richly concentrated in their heads, and by getting some of these the home village will divert a part of the current vitality into their own community. It is easy to see how the attacked group, after losing several heads—and with them some of their total stock of magical power—will at once begin planning a return raid in order to get back what they have lost; in other words, to restore the

"balance of heads." Especially will they feel the need to do this if they begin to suffer misfortunes after the raid. A good stock of heads is the glory of a native Borneo settlement. In the early days of white contact, the people proudly displayed their skull collections to European officials, and were dumfounded when the reaction was not one of congratulation. (Kennedy, 1942:101)

That these ideas about the magical power of heads were held also by the Ibans specifically is indicated in St. John's discussion of the feasts of the Ibans:

The object of them all is to make their rice grow well, to cause the forest to abound with wild animals, to enable their dogs and snares to be successful in securing game, to have the streams swarm with fish, to give health and activity to the people themselves, and to ensure fertility to their women. *All these blessings, the possessing and feasting of a fresh head are supposed to be the most efficient means of securing.* The very ground itself is believed to be benefited and rendered fertile . . . (St. John, 1863:I, 204; italics mine).[1]

An important implication of these ideas is that headhunting is an appropriate response to misfortunes: insofar as the very occurrence of misfortunes signals a shortage of magical power, men must respond with attempts to get more of the heads in which resides the power for warding off further misfortunes. Keeping in mind the appropriateness of this response in the people's own view, we can see how headhunting could have worked in a multiphase process responding to perturbations among the Ibans or among other headhunters holding similar ideas. Hit by a misfortune, Group A takes a head from neighboring Group B. Following this, B may attempt to restore the "balance of heads" with a headhunting raid against A or some other group. (That the balance did not have to be sought in the form of a head specifically from A is suggested in the case of Iban headhunting by nineteenth century statements to the effect that the Ibans of the Saribas and Skrang rivers did not make any selection of victims "except a selection of those who are not strong enough to resist them" [Devereux, 1855:24]). If A does in turn lose a head to B, this may be regarded as a new misfortune requiring a new head to be taken—although not necessarily from B. If, on the other hand, A loses no head and suffers no other misfortune for an extended period, then it is possible for A to avoid escalation into later phases of the multiphase process.

PLATE 8   Iban War Leader with His Head Trophy, Second Division

The later phases are distinguishable on the basis of the more intense or frequent headhunting associated with them. By suffering persistent or repeated misfortunes during relatively short periods, a group—let us again call it A—moves into these phases. Because of the misfortunes, A now has to keep taking heads and it turns to the weakest of its neighboring groups as the easiest sources for these. Groups that are repeatedly and increasingly the victims of headhunting raids eventually abandon their lands and move off to somewhere else. If A, although successful in headhunting, has itself been greatly weakened by the misfortunes it has suffered, it may ignore the abandoned lands. However, if it has not been so weakened and if the persistence or recurrence of its misfortunes has resulted from population pressure—for example, crop failures because of overexploitation of the land or deaths, disease, and infertility because of food shortages and related stresses— A then finds release from adversity by taking over the lands of its erstwhile victims, an action which is the culmination of the multiphase process.

The process described in the preceding two paragraphs is not something that can be illustrated with detailed accounts of historical sequences in which a long series of headhunting raids by Ibans exerting increasing pressure on their existing territory is followed by a release from the pressure through their annexation of the land of their victims. The limited available evidence concerning the Ibans in the eighteenth century and earlier is, however, consistent with a process operating generally as described. Thus, the Ibans' oral traditions make clear on the one hand that Iban groups were taking both heads and land from their neighbors long before Brooke reached Sarawak and, on the other hand, that territorial expansion was slow among the Ibans (which is what we would expect if the tempo of the process were dependent on the cumulative effects of localized headhunting raids in response to misfortunes). According to the traditions recorded by Sandin (1968), a spread from Iban homelands in the interior Kapuas basin of Kalimantan began about sixteen generations ago, i.e., in about the middle of the sixteenth century.[2] Lands were occupied by the expanding Ibans first along the main rivers in the interior of Sarawak's Second Division and then up these rivers to the headwaters and downriver toward the coast. Summarizing the traditions describing the process whereby Ibans wrested territory from the Bukitans, Serus, and other mainly nomadic hunting and gathering peoples of the Second Division, Sandin notes that the "emphasis is upon essentially *local* affairs, or contacts between close neighbours." When Iban invasions are recounted, they are described as slow processes—"beginning by and large in the lower reaches of the river . . . and working gradually toward the head waters" (Sandin, 1968:59; italics his). Although the distance from the homelands in the Kapuas to the Sarawak coast is less than 100 miles, Ibans are not known to have made effective contacts with the coastal peoples until about seven to nine generations ago, i.e., in the middle or latter part of the eighteenth century. Consistent with this is a lack of references to the Ibans in the pre-nineteenth century documents of the Brunei Sultanate, which, before James Brooke became rajah of Sarawak, had included at least nominally some of the Iban country in the Second Division (Pringle, 1970:43–44). It is true that the Brunei documents available to scholars are scanty, but references to the Ibans in them might nevertheless be expectable if the Ibans' sphere of headhunting operations had not generally been of a localized character in the Sarawak interior.

The other motives for Iban headhunting which have been noted by authors in the nineteenth and twentieth centuries could all have been operating in earlier times without interfering with the process involving headhunting in response to misfortunes. Indeed, one of the motives, said to be an ancient one (Sandin, 1962, cited in Pringle, 1970:22–23), clearly provided further stimulus to headhunting in response to misfortunes when the misfortunes were those of death. This motive was the desire to terminate mourning periods during which bereaved spouses could not remarry, other kin of the deceased could not wear good clothes or finery, and all members of the local group or longhouse community were subject to certain other lesser ritual restrictions; a fresh human head is said to have been required for the ceremony ending the mourning period (Pringle, 1970:22–23; see also Beccari, 1904:47; Horsburgh, 1858:13; Leach, 1965:166–167; St. John, 1879:195, Note 2).

Another motive, related to the release of tensions, was described as follows by Odoardo Beccari, an Italian naturalist who "wandered" in Borneo in the 1860s: "Not infrequently a Dyak [Iban] starts on a head-hunting expedition by himself, as a relaxation or to wear off the effects of a domestic squabble, just as with us a man might go out rabbit-shooting to get over an attack of ill-humour" (Beccari, 1904:47). Insofar as any such headhunting for tension-release would, it may be argued, have become more frequent with increase in the tensions generated by such concomitants of population pressure as a diminishing per-capita food supply and increasing intragroup competition for resources, the kind of headhunting referred to by Beccari may be regarded as compatible with the operation of the previously described multiphase process.

Something which nineteenth century writers emphasized and tended to regard as an independent motivation for headhunting is the desire for the prestige that accrued to the successful headhunter and, more specifically, the desire for the esteem of young women who were being courted (see the section on "Women's Influence," pp. 163–166 in the chapter on "Head-Hunting" in Roth, 1896:II; also, Earl, 1837:266–267; Hornaday, 1890:465; Keppel, 1846:35–36; Keppel, 1853:I, 129; Moor, 1837:9 [note], 52). There is no reason to suppose, however, that the young men could not have been satisfying such desires by engaging in headhunting when mourning periods needed to be ended or when the occurrence of misfortunes was signaling a community need for more magical power. Indeed, the rewards of prestige are likely to have been all the greater when the young men were meeting group needs with their headhunting. In other words, prestige motives could have been ancillary to the other motives mentioned.[3]

Another possibility is that headhunting raids were consciously undertaken in order to obtain land. That this was sometimes the case in the latter part of the nineteenth century is suggested by Freeman (1970:150, note), who remarks that the Ibans in the upper Rejang basin were invaders and not only took heads from enemies but also attempted to force their abandonment of territory by such measures as burning down their longhouses and destroying their implements. As might be expected, evidence is deficient for earlier periods, but Sandin (1968:18) does provide one account in which an Iban leader, living 14 or 15 generations ago, declared war on the Bukitans whom he wished to drive out of a reputedly very fertile area which he desired for his own people. It may be supposed that the war which was declared was to consist of headhunting raids, but this is not explicitly stated. In any event, the possibility that Iban headhunters sometimes became aware that not only getting heads but also getting land might be a means of ending their misfortunes—just as Maori warriors sometimes made land as well as revenge the object of their fighting (see Chapter 4)—is in no way incompatible with the existence of a process in which the antecedents of territorial conquests were localized headhunting raids in response to misfortunes that had increased as the result of population pressure.

HEADHUNTING FAR AND ITS EFFECTS

One thing for which the evidence is quite clear is that there was in Sarawak's Second Division, particularly among the Iban tribes of the Saribas and Skrang rivers, a change in the late eighteenth or early nineteenth century from localized to extensive headhunting. This change will first be described, and then we will consider why it took place and how, it af all, it could be disruptive to the kind of system which was described in the preceding section.

When gradual territorial expansion finally brought some Ibans into continuing contact with the coastal areas of the Second Division about seven to nine generations ago, the settlements they found there were composed of people usually described in the literature on Sarawak as "Malays." It should be understood, however, that instead of necessarily being the descendants of migrants from peninsular Malaysia or Sumatra, these coast-dwellers were, by and large, the descendants of various tribal peoples of Borneo and were called "Malay" by virtue of their being followers of Islam (Pringle, 1970:xviii–xix). Ibans both joined existing Malay settlements and established new settlements in the lower reaches of the Second Division rivers, so that, by the time of James Brooke's advent, each river system had Malay-dominated communities at the coast, settlements of Malays and Ibans living together in more or less equal numbers in a middle zone, and wholly pagan Iban communities in the interior (Pringle, 1970:52).

Once settled in the lower reaches of the rivers, Ibans encountered some enemies different from those whom they had previously fought and whose heads they had previously taken. These were the notorious Illanun pirates, who, from their homeland in Mindanao and from bases in northern Borneo and elsewhere, were marauding in big swift prahus throughout maritime southeast Asia. According to traditions (Sandin, 1968:63–64), it was as a defense against the Illanuns that the first large warboat of the Ibans was constructed. This was done by a leader named Unggang, who lived seven generations ago and, initially, used the boat, which could carry as many as 100 warriors, to prevent the Illanuns and other pirates from sailing up the Saribas River. Meeting with some success in this, he switched from defense to offense and began to attack trading ships and other vessels in the South China Sea and to take the heads of their crew members. This may have been the beginning of what was later described as Iban "piracy." In time, other Ibans built similar long, paddle-powered craft (see the description in Low, 1848:216–218) and by the 1820s, as Pringle (1970:48) notes, warboats of Saribas and Skrang Ibans were the scourge of much of the northwest coast of Borneo. By this time, some of the ways of the Illanun had been learned by Ibans, not only as their enemies, but also, to some extent, as their apprentices; ambitious young Ibans served on Illanun prahus cruising and raiding as far away as the Gulf of Thailand and the Vietnamese coast (Pringle, 1970:50–51 and 50, Note 4; cf. Orang Kaya Dana Makota's testimony in *Reports*, 1855:183).

It may be noted in passing that it would be a mistake to think that the Sarawak coast had always or continually been a theater of operations for pirates and that therefore it was in some sense predestined that Ibans would become involved in maritime marauding whenever their gradual expansion from the interior finally brought some of them to the coast. Actually, although there had certainly been piracy in the area previously, it did not become endemic in Borneo waters and elsewhere in the Indonesian archipelago until the latter part of the eighteenth century. By this time, restrictive Dutch trade policies, involving the compulsory stapling of commerce at Dutch ports such as Batavia and interference with the traffic of other entrepôts, had contributed to an upsurge of piracy in at least two ways. On the one hand, Malay rulers, deprived of resources and revenues from peaceful commerce, increased their marauding activities, and, on the other hand, the weakening of the power of the sultanates allowed formerly subject peoples such as the Illanun to set themselves up as independent communities of freebooters.[4] Some Illanuns had in fact been observed by William Dampier in 1686 to be a peaceful people involved in exchanging gold and beeswax from the Mindanao interior for goods available at the coast (Dampier, 1968:222–223, 228). According to a later European voyager, it was not until about 1770 that Illanuns established bases on the west coast of Borneo after their home districts in Mindanao had been devastated by a volcanic eruption (Forrest, 1780:192). Men from these newly founded bases are likely to have been among the pirates encountered by Ibans reaching the Sarawak coast in the latter part of the eighteenth century. It can be seen thus that a rather fortuitous conjunction of what had been separate series of historical events was responsible for the sudden enlargement of the world of some Ibans and for their turning to piracy.

As "pirates," however, the Ibans were unusual, for they persisted in something absent from the behavioral repertoire of Illanun and Malay marauders: taking heads. An article by Dalton in a Signapore newspaper in 1827 noted that a condition of the Ibans' connection with the veteran pirates was that victims' heads were the prize of the Ibans (in Moor, 1837:9, note; the author is identified in *Reports,* 1855:170–171), and similar observations were made by later writers (e.g., Low, 1848:189; St. John, 1863:I, 78; cf. *Reports,* 1855:34 and *passim*). When the Ibans organized their own maritime raids and also, later, when they were used by extortion-minded Malay chiefs on expeditions against communities of Land Dayaks and other people in the Sarawak interior, some plunder (brassware, guns if available, gold, silver) was taken but the Ibans' major objective still was getting heads (Keppel, 1853:I, 129; Low, 1848:189–190; *Reports,* 1855; St. John, 1863:I, 78–80). Undoubtedly some of the headhunters eventually became accomplished plunderers (*Reports,* 1855:34–35 and *pas-*

sim), but, as late as the 1830s, Iban raiders were ignoring "large quantities of rich merchandise" and were content with the heads of their victims, along with some iron and "trifles" (Earl, 1837:269, describing an Iban attack on a Chinese settlement near the mouth of the Sambas River in Kalimantan).[5] It is not surprising that in the controversies that raged in England in the early 1850s about Rajah James Brooke's actions in Borneo and particularly about the massacre of hundreds of Skrang and Saribas Ibans at the Battle of Beting Marau in 1849, a key issue could be whether or not these Ibans were indeed pirates (Irwin, 1955: Chap. 7, especially p. 141; Pringle, 1970: Chap. 3; Runciman, 1960: Chap. 4; *Reports*, 1855:21–39 and *passim*; and Tarling, 1963: Chap. 3). On the one hand, Brooke's opponents were able to argue with some cogency that the people were not "pirates by profession" and that their so-called piracies were essentially headhunting expeditions (Chamerovzow, [1851]: 21, 25; see also Hume, 1853, and *Reports*, 1855:*passim*). And even Henry Keppel (1853:I, 129), who had led British naval forces in attacks on the Saribas and Skrang tribes in 1843 and 1844 and was one of Brooke's defenders, noted that the Ibans, intent "above all on heads" as they went forth on their expeditions, were different from other pirates and that the character of piracy had been "altered, and rendered more bloody, by the infusion of this Dyak [Iban] element." On the other hand, Keppel also remarked that Iban boats "swept the seas, and devastated the shores" of Borneo over considerable distances, and such an observation, made also by others who noted Iban maritime expeditions as far south as Pontianak in Kalimantan (*Reports*, 1855:160, 166, 198, 199, 211–212) and at least as far north as Mukah in Sarawak's Third Division (*Reports*, 1855:215–216), was clearly at odds with the insistence of Brooke's adversaries that the Ibans' attacks were no more than traditional warfare among neighboring tribes (Chamerovzow, [1851]:19–21, 25; Hume, 1853:17–18; *Reports*, 1855:31 and *passim*).[6]

In actuality, what the Saribas and Skrang Ibans were engaging in was neither "piracy as a profession" nor traditional intertribal hostilities. Their unprofessional character as pirates is indicated not only by the arguments presented by Brooke's opponents—for example, that real pirates go out from ports in "fine fast-sailing, well built, well-armed vessels, not in small boats that paddle along the coast"

(Robert Hentig's testimony in *Reports,* 1855:128). There is also the fact that, in contrast to such pirates as the Illanuns who often cruised for two or more years in fleets of 15 to 20 prahus and shifted their theaters of operation according to the availability of food and plunder (*Reports,* 1855:151; cf. James Brooke's memorandum in Keppel, 1846:307), Iban groups never appear to have abandoned the farms of their home communities and to have made raiding their main activity. Instead, they often made their expeditions in agricultural slack seasons—either after clearing and planting or after harvesting their rice (*Reports,* 1855:110, 134; cf. Gomes, 1911:76 and, on the Ibans' annual agricultural cycle, Freeman, 1970:241–242)—and customarily returned home after a single successful attack (Spenser St. John's testimony in *Reports,* 1855:201). The Ibans depended for their livelihood on their farms, not on their raids.

Moreover, it may be noteworthy that after successful attacks the full-fledged pirates of maritime southeast Asia kept some of their victims for ransom or for sale as slaves and apparently did not as a rule put the others to death (Anonymous [J. Crawfurd?], 1825:245). To the extent that it was in the interest of these pirates to spare the lives of their victims in order to be able to prey upon them again at a later time,the sheer bloodiness of some of the Iban raids may have been inconsistent with piracy as a continuing profession. C. F. Bondriot, a Dutch official testifying in Singapore before the Royal Commission investigating Rajah Brooke in 1854, remarked:

> All the natives on the west coast are all aware of these [Saribas and Skrang Iban] tribes, and fear them; they are different from the other native pirates, who go all round the island. They do not kill you at once, should you wish to surrender, but in the end you are sure to be beheaded . . . . I know one instance where they killed about 400 . . . (*Reports,* 1855:110).

Other raids in which Ibans in warboats attacked river villages and killed and beheaded 100 or more of the inhabitants were described by witnesses at the Singapore inquiry (e.g., Moosah's testimony in *Reports,* 1855:177 and St. John's testimony in *Reports,* 1855:201), and accounts were also given of the killing and decapitation of the entire crews of Malay trading prahus (e.g., the testimonies of Dato Patingi and Nakodah Mahomed in *Reports,* 1855:138, 186).

The large, unwieldy prahus sailing between Singapore and the Oya and Mukah districts of Sarawak's Third Division were, according to St. John (1879:162), an especially easy prey for the headhunters in their warboats; when the Ibans took these prahus by surprise, nobody in them would survive, and, when a surprise failed, the vessels "would be run ashore, and the men rush into the jungle to escape from their bloodthirsty pursuers." The Ibans did on occasion take prisoners whom they either disposed of as slaves to their Malay associates or, in the case of some women and young children, kept for themselves and often eventually adopted into their own groups (Low, 1848:200–201; Pringle, 1970:28; *Reports,* 1855:156 [William Napier's testimony], 225 [James Brooke's testimony]; Roth, 1896:II, 209–210; St. John, 1879:209). Apart from this, however, killing and taking heads with abandon were the rule, and almost entire districts were desolated as a result of Iban raids (Keppel, 1846:341; *Reports,* 1855:187; St. John, 1879:162–163).

If then the Ibans on the coast were engaging neither in "piracy as a profession" nor in traditional intertribal hostilities, what were they doing? Clearly, it was headhunting, but it was headhunting without moorings, headhunting directed as readily against distant Chinese towns in the Dutch territories as against neighboring groups whose land might eventually be taken in the culmination of a multiphase response process.[7] Why had this extensive headhunting developed? Part of the answer must lie in the relative ease with which Ibans from the Saribas and Skrang rivers could obtain heads from the coastal areas in the late eighteenth and early nineteenth centuries. Presumably the earlier localization of Iban headhunting in the interior of Borneo was the result of the fact that the most readily available victims were those in neighboring pagan groups. When, however, Ibans settled the Saribas and Skrang rivers, they found themselves removed from their traditional sources of heads. According to St. John's testimony at the Singapore inquiry (*Reports,* 1855:205), the nearest interior tribe from whom heads could be taken were the Bugaus, at a month's journey by foot from the settlements of the Saribas and Skrang tribes. These two tribes were allies and were themselves in control of large tracts of country, and, at this time, members of the tribes could not take one another's heads.[8] In the case of the Saribas people, there were some expeditions against settlements of Bukitans and Serus along tributaries of the Krian River (which is not far from the coast), but the Ibans were met with determined opposition by some of these people, especially by some Seru groups (Sandin, 1968:52–53, 76–77). Further to the east, rugged hills contributed to the isolation of the Saribas from interior areas (cf. Pringle, 1970:207).

By contrast, there were coastal areas which could be readily reached by boat and, moreover, presented good opportunities for head-taking in the late eighteenth and early nineteenth centuries, opportunities resulting to a large degree from the disorder along Borneo's western coast during this period. This disorder stemmed partly from the previously mentioned decline in the power of the Malay sultanates as a result of restrictive Dutch trade policies. In the absence of the control that had formerly been exercised from Brunei, local Malay chiefs in Sarawak vied with one another for power and sought to attract both Illanun pirates and Iban marauders to their cause. Further south, Dutch vessels policed the coast to a limited extent until the beginning of the nineteenth century, but, when Holland became a vassal-state of Napoleon's empire, her ships were attacked by British ones and were kept for some years from the East Indies. The British, already burdened by the European war, did not in turn take up the role of policing the Eastern Seas. After restoration of the Dutch in the region in the post-Napoleonic period, they became weakened by a war which broke out in Java in 1825 and they progressively cut down their establishments in western Borneo. By this time, the Chinese who had come as gold miners in the middle of the eighteenth century were accepting the authority of neither Malays nor Dutch and were living in independent self-governing communities.[9]

In the absence of any authorities capable of coordinating either resistance to attackers or retaliation upon them, the Saribas and Skrang Ibans, belonging to the two largest and most powerful Iban tribes near the coast (St. John, 1879:161–162; cf. Pringle, 1970:15), could make their raids upon individual settlements or upon small parties at sea with impunity. There was an advantage for them in the sheer terror that headhunting produced initially among such people as the Malays and Chinese, not previously subjected to the practice. The fearsome reputation which the Saribas and Skrang Ibans acquired extended as far north as Brunei and as far south as Pontianak in Kalimantan (*Reports*, 1855:110, 167, 168, 175, 176, 179, 189, 197, 199, 216) and had the effect that people learned to run away on merely seeing these Ibans, for, it was thought, otherwise the result would surely be decapitation (Moosah's testimony in *Reports*, 1855:179). Even children all along the coast expressed great fear when the name of the Saribas and Skrang Ibans was heard (C. F. Bondriot's testimony in *Reports*, 1855:110). Embroideries were made on the headhunters' reputations, and such customs as hauling in people with long hooks attached to poles and then cutting their throats were attributed to them (Hajee Mahomet Sahat's testimony in *Reports*, 1855:199).

In particular places or among particular people, some resistance to the Ibans did in time develop. Fishermen in the Mukah River sounded alarms when the headhunters approached and war prahus were maintained for defensive purposes at the Mukah settlements (*Reports*, 1855:216–217). Some people went to sea only in large parties so as to avoid encountering Ibans without having sufficient numbers to resist them (*Reports*, 1855:197). And trading prahus carried leelas (brass guns) with which Iban marauders could sometimes be repulsed—especially, of course, when the attackers' own arms were inferior (see the examples in *Reports*, 1855:180, 190, 192–193, 196).

All of these, however, were defensive measures. Prior to the expeditions organized by the British in the 1840s, the non-Iban coastal communities victimized by the Saribas and Skrang tribes avoided retaliating. They were, according to witnesses at the Singapore inquiry, too afraid (*Reports*, 1855:132, 166, 191, 199). The only exception before Rajah Brooke's arrival appears to have occurred when some Malays and Land Dayak tribesmen joined together and took their prahus to the mouth of the Saribas River, but even such forces, equipped with guns and large vessels, did not dare to enter the Saribas country and could effect only temporary blockades to prevent Iban raiders from coming out to sea (testimonies of Dato Patingi and Moosah in *Reports*, 1855:132, 178). Consistent with this is testimony given at the Singapore inquiry to the effect that other tribes would have the courage to retaliate against the Saribas only if the Malays would join them (Nakodah Hajee Achmet's testimony in *Reports,* 1855:191). The Malays, however, as will be discussed more fully below, were more ready to join with the Ibans than to join against them. Commissioner Devereux's conclusion from the Singapore inquiry was that no enemies of the Saribas and Skrang Ibans penetrated their country, located some distance inland from the coast, until the British expeditions did so after 1840 (*Reports,* 1855:24). This is not quite true, for other Ibans from coastal areas of the First Division and parts of the Second Division south of the Lupar River sometimes made headhunting raids against Saribas (Sandin, 1968:65 ff.; see also Brooke's Journal for August 30, 1839 in Keppel, 1846:35–36; Pringle, 1970:46–47), but these more traditional enemies apparently did not have the manpower for major or sustained attacks. By not having to devote themselves to defense on their own ground, the Saribas and Skrang Ibans remained free to direct their raids against new victims who had not developed effective defensive measures. The only selection of victims made by the headhunters was "a selection of those . . . not strong enough to resist them" (Reports, *1855*:24).[10] With hundreds of miles of coasts and rivers along which they could range and make attacks when circumstances seemed favorable, the Ibans had in the coastal areas a supply of easily available victims that was apparently far from being exhausted by the time of James Brooke's arrival in Sarawak.[11]

The role of the Malays in these proceedings deserves some special comment. The elite among the Malays of northwest Borneo in the nineteenth century were Brunei nobles, holding the title *pengiran,* and so-called Arabs, ostensibly of Arab blood and distinguished by the title *sharif* or *sayid.* Beneath them in rank was a diverse class of local chiefs closely identified with particular rivers. These chiefs, even if acknowledging the formal suzerainty of Brunei, sent little or no tribute there. A Malay lower class included fishermen and rice farmers, but, as Pringle (1970:60) notes, these were not numerous enough, particularly in the Iban country, to constitute a substantial peasantry of the sort which was to be found in peninsular Malaysia. The absence of such a peasantry is significant, for it meant that the political and commercial power of Malay nobles or aristocrats in Sarawak depended on the support of pagan communities. In rivers or river systems with numerous Ibans, it was advantageous for the Malay chiefs to woo the Ibans rather than oppose them. And the chiefs could try to augment their power by getting the Ibans to raid either against rival chiefs and their supporters (including other Ibans) or against pagans who did not have the Ibans' headhunting propensities and could be subjected to exactions of goods and services. The Ibans were amenable to such collaboration because there were things that they wanted from the chiefs, particularly the salt and the salt fish which were traded for Iban rice. However, Ibans never gave their support to such a degree as to enable any one Malay noble or aristocrat or group of chiefs to gain control over a wide region or to institute an effective trade monopoly. In other words, no Malays could become strong enough to impose oppressive terms of trade upon the Ibans. By not uniting in the support of any Malay chiefs, the headhunters could maintain their supply both of trade goods and of heads. An epitomization of this pattern of interaction— a "delicate pattern," says Pringle (1970:64)—was provided by Charles Brooke, the second white rajah, in remarks made about the Kanowit Ibans in 1856:

> They loved independence . . . and as these two requirements [for heads and salt] could not be found in the same quarter they, in former times, usually made peace with one petty Malay chief for the purpose of obtaining salt, while the heads were brought from some other petty Malay chief's village lying in another direction. (Brooke, 1866:I, 159–60)[12]

All the evidence of the relative ease with which Ibans could obtain heads in the coastal areas still leaves the question of what made the Ibans want the heads. In other words, are the same motivations to be attributed to the headhunters when their operations were localized and when they were not? Clearly some of the coastal raids were, for at least some of the participants, responses to misfortunes, particularly deaths. Abdulkassim, a Malay trader and teacher, stayed briefly with Rentap, a renowned Skrang leader, in the 1840s. The following is the answer that Abdulkassim gave when he was asked at the Singapore inquiry whether Rentap had "any cause of quarrel with any of the tribes he attacked": "He did not mention any cause; there was no other cause but the desire of heads. If a relation of

Rantap [Rentap]—his father, mother, or wife—should die, they go out on an expedition for heads. It is a relief to his feelings, and he is satisfied" (*Reports*, 1855:181; cf. Note 3, *supra*). In a similar vein, St. John once met the most influential Saribas chief and found that he was "dressed in nothing but a dirty rag around his loins, and thus he intended to remain until the mourning for his wife should be terminated by securing a head" (St. John, 1863:I, 82).

A possibility not to be ruled out is that some of the misfortunes to which Ibans responded with coastal raids were related to growing population pressure. In 1848, the year of his arrival in Sarawak as James Brooke's secretary, St. John estimated that the Saribas and Skrang tribes each had about 6,000 fighting men (St. John, 1879:161). By this calculation, the total population of the two tribes must have been several times 12,000 and would have been capable, at least in particular localities, of exerting considerable pressure upon the land. Unfortunately (although not surprisingly) the detailed demographic and ecological data that would be needed to test such possibilities are not available. It may, however, be noteworthy that soils of the Second Division are reported to be generally poor (Pringle, 1970:11, Note 2) and that there were migrations of Saribas and Skrang Ibans northward to the Kanowit River system in the 1840s and 1850s (Brooke, 1866:I, 327). The migrations were partly a fleeing from Rajah Brooke and the British, but they may also have been prompted to some degree by exhausted soils and population pressure in the home districts.

However, while the possible influence of population pressure upon coastal headhunting raids by the Saribas and Skrang tribes in pre-Brooke times is not to be ruled out, it is not something that we need to make much of in order to develop the argument in this chapter. In light of the ease with which headhunting victims could be found in the coastal areas, we need not even insist on regarding misfortunes as the most likely triggers for Saribas and Skrang raids. Another possibility is that a custom of saving potential victims for the times of misfortune or crisis when heads would clearly be needed was continued by Ibans and similarly motivated headhunters only so long as the number of people whose heads might be taken was distinctly limited and so long as taking their heads was an enterprise rendered dangerous by the likelihood that members of the victims' group would retaliate. In other words, motives which, under more constrained circumstances, were only ancillary—for example, perhaps the Iban young men's desire for prestige and feminine affection—could become the main reasons for headhunting as the number of potential victims became less limited. Moreover, there might be involved a newly appropriate rationale whereby the greater the number of heads taken, the less danger would there be of misfortunes. Although this rationale, which might be designated the rationale of "preventive" headhunting, is not mentioned in the better known discussions of Borneo headhunters, it has been attributed to other people, such as the Wa of Upper Burma (Scott, 1900:501), who believed in taking heads when misfortunes struck. It is possible also that many of the Saribas and Skrang men felt no need for rationales; it was enough for them to engage in headhunting because of the adventure involved and because they knew the activity to be a good thing and the custom of their ancestors.[13]

There could be much further speculation on the motives for coastal raiding, but it is not needed for proceeding to the question of the effects of the extensive headhunting upon the traditional multiphase response process. In the Maori case to be described in the next chapter, there ultimately was breakdown and abandonment of the whole war process after revenge-seeking, comparable in its traditional functions to Iban headhunting, became nonlocalized in the early years of the nineteenth century. The question, then, is whether extensive headhunting was leading to similar effects.

In answer, it may be argued that it was not and that a critical difference between the Iban and Maori cases is that headhunting, unlike revenge-seeking, did not become costly in men and resources when it became nonlocalized. Of course, it may have been costly for some of those whom the Saribas and Skrang Ibans attacked, but what is significant is that for the attackers themselves it did not become costly at all in pre-Brooke times and, as we shall see, even after Brooke's advent the costs were heavy only intermittently and for a brief period. Before the 1840s, as previously noted, the headhunters' agricultural pursuits were not interfered with; victims were readily available; defenses against retaliatory expeditions were not required;

and there were such bonuses as plunder and the trade goods from Malay collaborators.

It might be thought that the extensive headhunting had a hidden cost insofar as it prevented people from obtaining needed land by means of the operation of the traditional system, i.e., the land that would become available because of a neighboring enemy group's attrition and withdrawal as a result of its being subjected to *intensive* headhunting. Actually, although there seems to be no evidence that the Saribas and Skrang Ibans in the early nineteenth century prior to Brooke rule were taking land from the victims of their coastal marauding, some of the weaker coastal groups preyed upon by the headhunters during this period were, as previously noted, abandoning their lands. Accordingly, we should not rule out the possibility that the Ibans would eventually have annexed these territories or, as previously discussed, that some of the Saribas and Skrang raids in the early nineteenth century were responses to misfortunes related to population pressure. It seems likely, however, that some relief from whatever pressure there might have been was provided by the plundering, trading, service as sailors, and other activities in which Ibans could engage as a result of their contacts with the coast. Furthermore, it must be remembered that the period of extensive headhunting before Brooke came was relatively short—possibly not long enough for population pressure, even in the absence of new outlets, to have increased so much as to call for the annexation of new lands before the 1840s.

What happened after Brooke became rajah? A few times, the Saribas and Skrang were made to pay heavily for their coastal raids. Viewing the Iban depredations as inimical to the development of trade and effective government in northwest Borneo, Brooke was able to persuade Captain Henry Keppel and other naval commanders to regard the Ibans as pirates and therefore as appropriate quarry for the men, guns, and ships of the British navy. The expeditions of the 1840s, in which the navy acted in concert with Brooke and his Malay and pagan allies, resulted in the deaths of many hundreds of Saribas and Skrang tribesmen and the destruction of numerous habitations and boats. From but one battle in the 1849 expedition—the controversial Battle of Beting Marau, which led to intense debate in England and eventually to the Singapore inquiry—British sailors received bounty for having killed 500 "pirates."[14]

Witnesses at the Singapore inquiry maintained that the expeditions of the 1840s had a deterrent effect on the Saribas and Skrang Ibans (*Reports*, 1855:36–37 and *passim*), but, as a result of the controversies generated by the expeditions, Brooke was denied British naval support after 1849. The policy to which he then turned was the development of fortified downriver outstations commanded by his English officers and intended to keep Iban marauders from reaching the coastal areas. Beginning in the mid-1850s, this was augmented with another policy to be referred to later: the use of "pacified" downriver Ibans on punitive expeditions against defiant upriver ones.

Throughout the first decade and a half of white-rajah rule, the Ibans apparently were probing to ascertain whether there was to be any lasting change in the costliness of coastal headhunting. Thus, early in 1842 (prior to any of the British naval expeditions), James Brooke received several visits from Matahari, a Skrang leader. Part of the description from Brooke's journal follows:

> He began by inquiring if a tribe, either Sakarran or Sarebus [Skrang or Saribas], pirated on my territory, what I intended to do. My answer was, 'To enter their country and lay it waste.' But he asked me again, 'You will give me, your friend, leave to steal a few heads occasionally?' . . . . He recurred to this request several times . . . (Keppel, 1846:173).

After an expedition against the Saribas in 1843, Captain Keppel first led British naval forces against the Skrang in 1844. Less than two years later, Brooke was writing in his journal as follows:

> In the midst of the general prosperity and increasing happiness of the tribes within the territory of Sarawak, I have suddenly received information that the Sakarran Dyaks have again been at sea with a force of seventy prahus, and not less than 1200 men, perpetrating many ravages, burning villages, carrying off the women and children into slavery, and laying waste the country, wherever their arms could reach.
>
> This is truly heart-rending. It was not to be expected, that the single attack made on this river by Keppel should totally eradicate, from amongst a numerous and warlike population, the deep-rooted and often-indulged habit of piracy; and although a slight advance has been made in detaching some of their chiefs from this evil course, I find that measures of kindness and conciliation are entirely thrown away, and that it will be

necessary to give these pirates another severe lesson, and to convince
them that their haunts in the Sakarran river cannot protect them from my
own native fleet, when supported by the boats of the vessels of war on
the station (Brooke's journal, March 1, 1846, in Mundy, 1848:II, 82).

Brooke's hopes for help from British warships were not quickly
realized, and three years more passed without further British naval
action against the Saribas and Skrang. When Keppel called at Sarawak on his way to China at the end of February 1849, he found:

> The insolence of the pirates had by this time so increased, that they had
> sent the Rajah a message of defiance, daring him to come out against
> them, taunting him with cowardice, and comparing him to a woman.
> This tone of security in the Serebas was certainly rather to be lamented
> than wondered at: they had lately with impunity captured several trad-
> ing boats, devastated two rivers, burned three villages, and slaughtered
> at least four hundred persons,—men, women, and children. "Why does
> the navy sleep?" asks a published letter of this date, from Sara-
> wak . . . (Keppel, 1853:I, 138).

At the beginning of March, a large Saribas force, said to have
comprised between 60 and 120 boats, raided the Sadong River in the
rajah's territory in the First Division and took "upwards of one
hundred heads" (Keppel, 1853:I, 139–140; St. John in *Reports*,
1855:201). In July, the ships of the Royal Navy arrived, and the
massacre of Saribas and Skrang Ibans at the Battle of Beting Marau
ensued.

The effect of the losses at Beting Marau and the establishment of
the fortified outstations seems to have been a lull in coastal endeav-
ors by the Ibans, but, by 1853, they were trying again. The following
is from St. John's response when he was asked at the Singapore
inquiry in 1854 whether the Skrang and Saribas Ibans had given up
"their forage by sea" (*Reports*, 1855:203):

> They have not gone in large numbers, but they have attempted it. They
> were prevented once in January 1853. A fort was erected by Mr. Brereton
> a little way up the Sakarran river, for the purpose of protecting a portion
> of the Sakarrans who had abandoned piracy. The pirate force belonging
> to the other portion came down and fired into the fort. They sent only
> two bankongs ahead, which fired into the fort. The fire was returned by
> the fort, to the great apparent injury of their bankongs. They fled . . . .
> Two attacks have also been made on the fort at Kanowit—one about five
> months ago—both on a large scale. Many attempts have been made to get
> to sea, and in small numbers they have succeeded in doing so sometimes

by other channels. About four months ago five or seven Chinamen, with 700 dollars' worth of cargo, took out a clearance from Sarawak to Singa; they were not heard of again until it was reported that their heads were hanging up in a Dyak house in the interior of Serebas: this was heard from some neutral Sakarran Dyaks who have not declared against piracy.[15]

When the Ibans tested themselves against the cannonry of the outstation forts and found that they could not prevail, they desisted from further attempts at bringing war fleets downriver past the forts. The conclusion stated by Pringle (1970:94) is probably correct: "The new outstations, far more than the Battle of Beting Marau, put an end to the era of Iban coastal raiding."

But if the establishment of the outstations finally made extensive headhunting in the coastal areas too costly for the Ibans, the effects of this on Iban headhunting still differ in an important way from what will be described in the next chapter as the effects of increased costliness on Maori revenge-seeking after it had become nonlocalized. The difference relates to the Maori reliance on guns in warfare. The Ibans sometimes also used guns, supplied to them by Malay associates or obtained as plunder, but the Ibans had to direct no great efforts to getting the weapons, could raid successfully without them, and usually did so when fighting in the interior (St. John, 1879:205–206; cf. St. John's testimony in *Reports*, 1855:206–207). In New Zealand, the adoption of muskets by Maoris throughout the country made all warfare costly and made it impossible to restore to operation a multiphase response process involving localized hostilities. Merely getting and maintaining supplies of guns and ammunition were expensive in men and resources for the Maoris. And all combatants in all phases of fighting had to have guns, for if one side were not to use them, the other surely would. In this situation, an advantage accruing from the kind of multiphase process which we have been considering was denied to the people: the avoidance of overexpenditure of resources in response to misfortunes or pressures that are minor or transitory. As I have discussed at greater length elsewhere (Vayda, 1974), such avoidance can be critically important insofar as maintaining the capacity to respond adaptively to stresses means, among other things, leaving resources available for responding to future stresses after present ones have been dealt with.[16]

By contrast to the course of developments among the Maoris, not only was it the case that extensive headhunting in the coastal areas was, for quite a while, not costly for the Saribas and Skrang Ibans. It was also the case that when it finally did become costly, the Ibans remaining outside the areas under the control of Brooke and his officers could revert to intensive headhunting operating as part of a multiphase response process. In other words, the difference that we are pointing to is that the increased costliness of extensive hostilities entailed an increased costliness of *all* hostilities for the Maoris but not for the Ibans.

There were, of course, many Ibans—indeed, perhaps all except some Saribas and Skrang tribesmen—for whom the involvement in localized hostilities was a matter not of reverting to certain practices but simply of continuing with them. While the so-called pirates were active on the coast, other Ibans, further in Sarawak's interior, were gradually expanding northward into the basin of the Rejang River in Sarawak's Sixth Division and westward to tributaries of the Kapuas River in Kalimantan. Pringle (1970:252) notes that the early movements into the Rejang basin were generally only to the headwaters of the streams opposite the people's Second Division home rivers (Pringle, 1970:252), and he refers to headhunting raids by migrating Ibans against the groups whose land was being taken, especially along the nearer tributaries of the Kapuas (Pringle, 1970:253). With respect to the Iban movement into the Rejang, the role of headhunting is discussed also by Freeman (1970:150, note). Although these gradual migrations and headhunting raids in the interior continued after the advent of Brooke rule on the coast, we need to be but little concerned with them here insofar as many of the Ibans involved had not had the experience of extensive coastal marauding.

There is, however, some evidence about Ibans who had had that experience and about their reversion to localized hostilities. This is the kind of change to which Baring-Gould and Bampfylde (1909:155) were referring in their *History of Sarawak* when they wrote about Skrang pirates who, in consequence of no longer being able to shoot down to the sea in their warboats, were exerting their "mischievous energies in attacking the peaceful Dyaks in their districts." Some of these "peaceful Dyaks" were former allies and fellow tribesmen who,

PLATE 9   Skulls in Iban Longhouse, Second Division

by virtue of living closer to areas controlled by Brooke and his officers, had accepted the Europeans' government and had become enemies to headhunters from both the upper Skrang and the upper Saribas.[17] North of the Saribas River were other possible targets of headhunting raids: the Seru and Bukitan people previously mentioned. Although these might not have been preferred victims when it was easy for Saribas men to obtain heads from coastal people who could be reached from the sea, the situation changed when Brooke rule became effective at the coast. In Sandin's account, numerous Saribas raids upon the Serus and Bukitans in the 1850s are referred to (Sandin, 1968:77–79). Minor attacks upon the Serus had been taking place for several generations, but, as Sandin (1968:77) notes, it was not until "well after the arrival of the English Rajah" that the Saribas Ibans finally displaced the Serus from most of the district of the Krian River and its tributaries. Presumably this was the outcome of intensified Iban activities vis-a-vis the Serus after the extensive coastal headhunting had been checked. There were Saribas raids and, eventually, territorial conquests also along the Julau River and its branches in the Rejang basin. Skrang Ibans were raiding and moving northward too during the 1850s and after, but, unfortunately, it is not possible to trace the movements from the Skrang River in much detail (Sandin, 1968:81).

Headhunting did not cease even among the downriver Saribas and Skrang Ibans who had had to accept Brooke rule. They became a main part of the soldiery of the white rajahs, and their rewards for participation in the punitive expeditions organized by Charles Brooke and other English officers included, as in the days of collaboration with Malay pirates and extortion-minded chiefs, the heads of those attacked and killed.[18] The headhunting by these Ibans is clearly not to be regarded as a reversion to former practices. In terms of the distances covered, the government expeditions were more like the coastal marauding of pre-Brooke times than like traditional, localized headhunting raids. And while the annexation of new territory became feasible for some Ibans as a result of the expeditions, this was not the culmination of a regulated and escalating multiphase process. Instead it was the effect of initially massive applications of force (made possible by government sponsorship of the expeditions) against the people whose lands the Ibans would subsequently take.

Thus, in the so-called Great Kayan Expedition of 1863, Charles Brooke's force consisted of 500 large boats and 15,000 men, mostly Ibans (Brooke, 1866:II, 300). The expedition penetrated over 200 miles upriver in the Rejang basin and killed, burned, pillaged, and spread general devastation over a wide area, from which many non-Iban people were said to have fled and to have stayed away forever (see Freeman, 1970:134, 150 [note] and the citations in Pringle, 1970:132–133). Never again after this was there "serious resistance" by non-Iban inhabitants to the Iban occupation of the lower middle sections of the Rejang (Freeman, 1970:134). And, in the absence of such resistance, the Ibans could expand into new lands at a much more rapid rate than previously and, because of the ease with which they could move on, could use those lands in wasteful and destructive ways (described in Freeman, 1970:Chap. 6; cf. Smythies, 1949).[19] More than any of the coastal enterprises of the pre-Brooke period, the massive government-sponsored expeditions to the interior were disruptive to regulation of land use, territorial expansion, and population dispersion by means of a traditional multiphase process.

For details of the ultimate disruption of the traditional system and the final cessation of Iban headhunting, we would have to follow the course of northern Borneo history into the twentieth century. This will not be done here, since we have already gone as far as necessary for showing the effects of the extensive hostilities of the pre-Brooke period upon the traditional, localized response process. As we have seen, in the Iban case there was no increase in costliness and no disruption of the traditional process comparable to what happened in the Maori case. Just as the chapters on the Maoris and the Marings show that systemic processes can be maintained through long intervals between the times when they operate to counteract stresses such as those associated with population pressure, the present chapter shows that such a process can be maintained through intervals that are nonlocalized as well as long.

It may be of interest in closing this chapter to note that this finding has implications complementing criticisms of so-called culture-contact or acculturation studies in anthropology. Earlier studies in this genre were based on the assumption that the acculturative changes being investigated constituted a departure from the previously self-contained, self-sufficient, and isolated condition of a "primitive" or "traditional" society. Criticisms of these studies have consisted of arguments to the effect that extralocal relations are to be found among almost all primitive and traditional societies and that the attribution of autonomous functioning to such societies is therefore unwarranted (see, for example, Murphy, 1964; Lesser, 1959; 1961). These criticisms may be justified, but, as the analysis in this chapter implies, we need now to go beyond them and to ask questions about the articulation between local and extralocal relations. Within this category of questions are the ones which we have, in effect, been exploring in the present chapter: questions about how and for how long and to what extent there may be replacement of local relations by extralocal ones without permanent disruption of the systemic processes whereby the local relations—not only between people and their neighbors but also between them and their resources—are regulated.

Such questions are important ones in the study of stability and change in social and ecological systems and need to be pursued through analyses of data on the history of other peoples and their systems. We might, for example, look at other headhunters such as the Nagas of the Assam hills who usually fought among themselves and were still doing so in the latter part of the nineteenth century but are described as having "seized the opportunity of harrying the Assam plains during the chaotic conditions arising in [King] Gaurinath's reign in the early part of the nineteenth century" (Shakespear, 1914:211; cf. Mackenzie, 1884:556).[20] Or we might turn to other frontiers in the interior of the Asian mainland where "barbarians"— not necessarily headhunters—were interacting with more civilized peoples and were adjusting to oscillations between centralization and decentralization in the civilized empires by making raids and invasions when opportunities were favorable and staying beyond the frontiers when they were not (Lattimore, 1962:506 and *passim*). Or we might go further afield and look at peasant communities which have been making cyclical "alternative responses to changes in conditions of the outside market" (Wolf, 1955:463). Parallel and potentially significant inquiries may in fact be conducted about any people whose recourse to extralocal relations—not only raiding and warfare but also commercial activities—has ebbed and flowed.

4

MAORIS AND MUSKETS
A Disrupted Process

The New Zealand Maoris live and work now in peace as citizens of a modern nation, but they are a people who, like some North American Indian groups and the Zulu of Africa, first became famous as warriors. A great deal has been written about Maori warfare. Particularly those aspects which seemed strange to European observers—cannibalism, the taking of heads, fighting in order to avenge verbal insults—have been richly and conspicuously documented, but copious materials on other aspects have also been made available to various observers and students of Maori life in the two centuries since Captain Cook and other Europeans first landed in New Zealand. In this chapter the materials are used to indicate that a multiphase war process operated adaptively in relation to population pressure in pre-European times and to show how it later became maladaptive and, in effect, a source of novel perturbations for the Maoris.

WARFARE, LAND USE, AND REVENGE IN PRE-EUROPEAN TIMES

It is appropriate to deal first with the traditional setting of Maori warfare. The Maoris' ancestors, who had come in their canoes from the small, tropical islands of eastern Polynesia, had found in the temperate, continental land mass of New Zealand a new and challenging environment. At the time of Cook's arrival in 1769, the Maoris, after centuries of living in New Zealand and after having hunted the moa and other indigenous species of flightless birds to extinction, still were adapting to this environment and extending their exploitation of it.

Warfare was part of the system whereby this was effected in the late eighteenth century. The roughly 40 Maori tribes of New Zealand comprised, at this time, some 100,000 to 300,000 people, but a considerably larger population could probably have been sustained even without the introduction of European technology. A New Zealand geographer, Kenneth B. Cumberland, has gone so far as to say that a *million* Maoris could have been supported—"in view of the reserves of bird life, fish, forest fruit, and timber and of cultivable soil, and in view of the equipment at the disposal of the people, their skills, and their knowledge" (Cumberland, 1949:417). This is probably an exaggerated estimate, but the important point is simply that there still was unexploited or underexploited land where the Maoris could have hunted, fished, grown their sweet potatoes, or dug the fern roots which were a staple of their diet. What was the role of warfare in moving people to such land from territories where the pressure of population was greater? This is the question that we must focus on.

As long as growing tribes or subtribes were able to expand into virgin land adjoining areas already being used by them, the increase and spread of Maori population from its small beginnings in the early period of settlement could have taken place peacefully.[1] However, as soon as there were groups whose territory adjoined only the territory of other groups rather than any unoccupied land suitable for exploitation by Maori tools and techniques, there could have been a role for warfare. Expansion could have taken place among the kin-ship-organized, genealogy-conscious Maoris very much as it did among the Tiv of northern Nigeria, a people whose recognized technique for the expansion of land holdings was, as recorded by the anthropologist Paul Bohannan (1954:5), a simple one:

> Always, when you make new farms, clear land towards that man whose land bounds yours, but who is more distantly related to you. When he objects, you are thus assured of the largest possible supporting group in any litigation, argument, or fight which may develop, since all the people who are more closely related to you than to him will come to your aid instead of his.
>
> Thus, to ensure the support of one's entire minimal segment [corresponding to a Maori subtribe or, in some cases, a segment thereof], one expands one's holdings against the territory of the companion minimal segment. To ensure the support of both these minimal segments, one expands against the territory of a genealogically more distant lineage.

The expansion of the Tiv in all directions was still going on during Bohannan's term of field work, and the kinds of opportunities that Bohannan had for observing the process are, of course, denied to the student of Maori society. Yet there is evidence that expansion among the Maoris not only could have been but actually *was* similar in some significant respects. The influence of considerations of genealogical proximity in determining to whom aid would be given in Maori warfare is shown, for example, in a European trader's eye-witness account of fighting between two sections of the Nga Puhi tribe in 1837. The trader, J. S. Polack, noted that the Hokianga natives, arriving after the hostilities had begun, were sorely puzzled which of the two parties to join, as they were *equally* related to the two (Polack, 1838:II, 42). And it is known that conquests involving displacement of vanquished foes from their territories did in fact occur in pre-European New Zealand. There are numerous examples of this in the annals of Maori warfare and there are cases, too, of beaten and displaced groups which, in turn, became the vanquishers and displacers of yet other groups (see the citations in Vayda, 1960:110, 115). There is, in other words, evidence that there took place among the Maoris chain reactions of aggressive territorial expansion in which the more closely related people or groups supported one another against the less closely related and unrelated. The expansion of one group, by means of warfare, into the

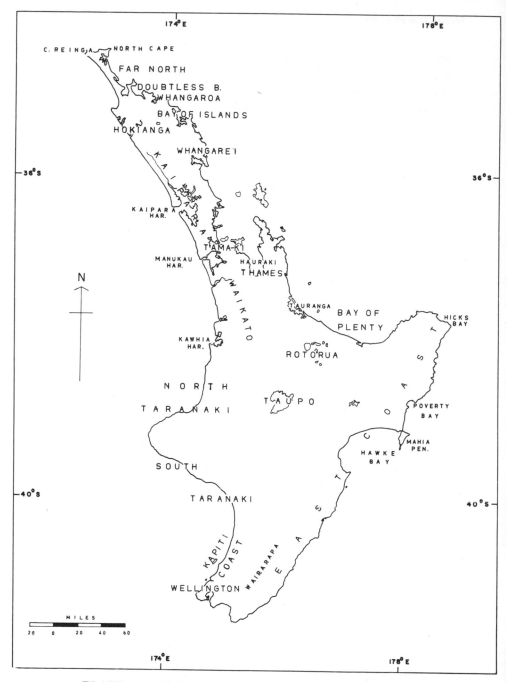

PLATE 10   Major Districts in the North Island of New Zealand

contiguous territory of another could lead the second group to expand into the contiguous territory of a third—and so forth until finally there would be displacement of a group having territory contiguous to unoccupied land.

At this point, we have already gone some way toward indicating the role of Maori warfare in maintaining the dispersion of people over the land and in making it possible for the population to continue to grow without overexploitation and degradation of particular localities. It remains to be shown, however, that the warfare was a multiphase process. By considering the Maoris' motivations for warfare, we not only can show this but also can underscore a point made in Chapter 2, namely, the importance of distinguishing between the factors affecting entry into war and those affecting escalation.

In the course of centuries, Maori warriors have no doubt had a considerable variety of individual, situationally determined, and idiosyncratic motives for taking up arms. We cannot be concerned with all of these, and it will be sufficient for our purposes to consider the two main, recurrent motives that the Maoris had for initiating war: acquiring land and revenging themselves upon groups that had committed offenses against them. The offenses provoking tribes or subtribes to seek vengeance included homicide or other violence, either by physical or fancied magical means, against members of the group (including women married to the offenders); trespass or poaching on food preserves claimed by the group; adultery with women of the group; theft of valuables; and insults to the group or, amounting to the same thing, to a chiefly member of it.

It has not been usual in discussions of Maori warfare to regard the land motive and the revenge motive as operating within a single process. Indeed, one scholar has gone so far as to suggest that each motive was characteristic of a different phase of Maori prehistory (Buck 1949:381, 387). This, however, is an interpretation inconsistent with the available evidence.[2] And it is possible to set forth an alternative interpretation whereby connections between the motives and between the fighting they lead to are indicated.

It must be noted first that the Maoris committing offenses that had to be avenged could thereby have often been, consciously or unconsciously, expressing the need of their groups for more territory.

This is perhaps most obviously so in the case of such offenses as trespass or poaching on other groups' food preserves, but murders and other physical assaults and even the insults could also result from the increasing pressure of population upon the land. A concomitant of this pressure would be a diminishing per-capita food supply and increasing intragroup competition for resources, both of which would contribute to domestic frustrations and other in-group tensions which might eventually find release in verbal or physical violence against members of other groups. Possible illustrations of this process are the examples that some authors give of a "peculiar custom" or "curious idea" of the Maoris: the murder of outsiders by someone who has been injured or aggrieved by members of his own group and who wishes therefore to "put his own people in the wrong" and thus make them subject to reprisals from the murder victims' groups (Gudgeon, 1885:28–29; Shortland, 1856:20; Tregear, 1904:326–327). However, the occurrences of this practice no doubt were rare, and many offenses were a way of giving vent to hostile or aggressive feelings without any deliberate intention of bringing the wrath of another group down upon one's own people.

The offended groups did not have to retaliate immediately.[3] They could bide their time, and, indeed, the memory of unavenged injuries was sometimes handed down from generation to generation, like an heirloom. When a Maori had an insult hurled at him, he could have recourse to the convention of wordlessly extending his arm above his head and closing the fingers as if clutching something. Or else he could utter some terse saying. Either action would signify that he would do something about the insult—but only later on.

Some groups, knowing themselves to be weak, tried no doubt to remain at home in peace rather than march against stronger groups that had insulted or injured them. But this policy would, in effect, be an invitation to the offending groups to continue with their offenses and to step up their frequency and magnitude. This is well expressed by a chief in one New Zealand writer's account of a Maori council of war: "To pass over such an unprovoked insult would be to end in the truth of the accusation of cowardice . . . . If we do not take revenge for this act of aggression they will become bolder, and it will be unsafe for us to move" (White, 1874:16–17). A weak group undertaking no retaliatory action might eventually be confronted on its home grounds with a powerful attacking force, consciously motivated now to annihilate or rout the group and to take over its territory. It must be said, however, that the policy of nonretaliation was not so futile as to make it inevitable that a particular enemy would escalate its offenses to this degree; it could also happen that the enemy would have its hands full with campaigns against other groups and it might even encounter some reverses rendering it incapable of mounting further attacks.

In any event, Maoris were strongly motivated to pursue policies of retaliation rather than nonretaliation. Suffering injuries meant to them a spiritual as well as a physical weakening and, accordingly, required the injured to strive to heal themselves by deeds that would restore their repute, their courage, their feeling of strength and wholeness. This way of thinking about injuries and about the necessity for avenging them is said to have been among the first lessons taught to Maori children. By the time the children were grown, they regarded revenge a vital point of honor and one of the most important duties of man—something to be pursued in spite of danger, difficulty, and every fatigue and privation. The ideas about revenge were what Gregory Bateson (1972:499–502) would call "hard-programmed": they were deeply ingrained and were accepted, without critical inspection, as a basis for other ideas and action.[4]

It seems likely then that unless a group was so weak as to make it impossible for its members to entertain some hope of success in a warlike enterprise, revenge would be sought by force of arms against offending groups. And the more that a group was offended against, the greater would be the incitement to its warriors to take arms and retaliate. The offenses would be recounted vehemently at public meetings which also featured inflammatory, warlike songs and chants and displays with weapons. The men would become eager to gird themselves with their flaxen war belts and set forth as a *taua toto*, a war party whose object is blood revenge for injuries received.[5]

How was this blood revenge to be obtained? After their initial shedding of blood, Maori war parties went on killing when they had the opportunity (see the section on "Pursuit and Mortality" in Vayda, 1960:83–92). However, they did not always have this oppor-

PLATE 11   Maoris in War Canoe (Drawn during Cook's First Voyage)

tunity and, moreover, when blood revenge was the object, this *could* be satisfied with the initial shedding of the enemy's blood. Indeed, according to some writers on Maori warfare, the procedure for avenging a murder was simply to proceed in secret to the offenders' place and there slay the first person encountered. By killing any member of the offenders' group, the warriors were obtaining revenge and could then return home with the satisfaction of a mission accomplished even if circumstances precluded their inflicting further bloodshed on their enemy (Thomson, 1859:I, 124; Buck, 1949:388). On the other hand, if circumstances permitted (if, for example, the enemy was completely surprised by the attack and could offer no initial resistance), the number of lives taken could be so great as to make it the enemy's turn to feel that it had to obtain vengeance by force of arms. This must have happened often, since a major part of Maori tribal histories consists of what one Maori scholar calls a "seesaw record of military exploits" (Buck, 1949:388).

The existence of this pattern of raids and counter-raids for revenge is what may have led some scholars to warn against thinking of Maori warfare in the same terms as warfare among so-called civilized peoples and even to suggest that "its psychology was more that of a seriously taken game" and that it might "almost be termed a manly physical exercise" (Beaglehole, 1940:63; Buck, 1924:364; cf. Best, 1924:II, 225). Certainly such characteristics as the small scale and short duration of active hostilities and the prominence of the revenge motive set Maori warfare apart from the type of warfare carried on by armies of state-organized societies. However, the contrasts must not be allowed to obscure the important similarities, as, for example, the fact that both types of warfare can result in territorial conquests and the redistribution of population. This admonition needs to be underscored, since just this kind of obscuring of similarities has taken place in the writings of numerous social scientists on the subject of primitive and modern or state-organized warfare (see, for example, Lesser, 1968:95; Steward and Shimkin, 1961:79; Wright, 1965:73–74).

We are speaking here about social scientists who have based their generalizations upon their reading of ethnography rather than upon their own field work, and it is possible that what has misled them into seeing only blood feuds and revenge and not territorial conquests in primitive warfare is something referred to earlier, namely, the general failure of ethnographers to note the connections between the fighting undertaken for revenge and the fighting undertaken for territory. The crucial observation which the ethnographers have not made is that the fighting for revenge, along with the offenses that give rise to it, can be part of a multiphase war process recurrently testing the manpower of groups—the manpower available for defending their land and using it. In this process, groups pass the first part of their tests by attacking when strongly provoked by insults or other injuries and by defending themselves stoutly when attacked. And as long as they are doing this, the war process that they are involved in can give the impression of having no relation to the conquest and use of land and being only a series of raids and counter-raids for revenge or glory or exercise. For such an impression to be corrected, it is necessary to take due notice of later phases of the process. Committing offenses and fighting for revenge are only the first part.

Following the process simply to a point where some groups fail to defend themselves or to retaliate adequately and their enemies, perceiving this, respond with conscious attempts to conquer their land is already sufficient to indicate a connection between fighting for revenge and fighting for territory. The process did not end, however, with outright attempts at taking land. If an attempt was successful to the extent that a group, having had a succession of victories over one section after another of a particular enemy tribe, was able to move into the territory of its beaten foe, some of the latter might still try to maintain a claim to the territory by "keeping their fires alight" somewhere within it, i.e., by keeping their cooking fires going and by digging fernroot, farming small pieces of ground, snaring birds, trapping rats, and pursuing other economic activities in some mountain or forest places not readily accessible to the conquerors. Such proceedings were intended by defeated people as a stopgap, something to be continued until they could reconstitute their forces and try to repossess their entire territory. Conquerors could achieve no recognized rights to taken lands without actually occupying them to the utter exclusion of the original owners,[6] and it could be a long time before they could be sure of having accomplished this. Defeated people sometimes spent years in refuge at the settlements of friends and relatives and then came to try to wrest their land back from the conquerors.[7]

A good illustration of how drawn out the process could be is provided by traditional accounts of the mid-eighteenth century conquest of the Auckland isthmus by the Ngati Whatua from further north. This tribe had earlier displaced the Wai o Hua people from the Kaipara district. It moved against them again on the Auckland isthmus in order to avenge some treacherous killings at a wake and some insults to a chief. The Ngati Whatua first defeated the people of a number of *pa* or fortified villages on the outskirts of the Wai o Hua country but then were driven back by their aroused enemies. After remaining for some time at their homes in Kaipara, the Ngati Whatua captured another Wai o Hua *pa* and then, by using the maneuver of a mock retreat which becomes a furious rally against unwitting pursuers, badly defeated the main body of the Wai o Hua. After feasting on the flesh of the enemy dead, the Ngati Whatua then attacked the principal Wai o Hua fortified village, which fell without much resistance. Fugitives from this and other villages fled southward; the Ngati Whatua were in possession of the Auckland isthmus. However, after an interval, many of the fugitives returned and reoccupied one of their *pa*. The Ngati Whatua delivered a dawn attack upon them and defeated them with great slaughter. Thereafter, the victorious warriors went back to Kaipara, probably in order to attend to subsistence labors. This emboldened some of the surviving Wai o Hua again, and they returned to their old homes. When the Ngati Whatua heard of this, they organized a new expedition, which moved by land and water against the three *pa* that the Wai o Hua had reoccupied. The *pa* were taken one after the other with much slaughter of the inmates. This finally completed the conquest of the Auckland isthmus. Surviving Wai o Hua remained thereafter as refugees with other tribes except for the few taken as slaves by the conquerors. The Ngati Whatua took over the Wai o Hua territory and were living there in peace when Captain Cook arrived in 1769.[8]

Among the things which the foregoing narrative shows in illustrating the drawn-out nature of the testing process is that it had

PLATE 12   Maori *Pa* in Pre-Musket Times

safeguards reducing the likelihood that groups with good fortune in war would take over land which they could exploit no better than could the vanquished. Military triumphs resulting from clever strategies or from luck could not lead to successful conquests if the victorious groups did not have the numbers and strength to use the defeated people's land and to resist their efforts to recover it.

We may say then, in summary, that the war process operating among the Maoris in pre-European times consisted of distinguishable phases of fighting for revenge, fighting for land, and territorial conquests and that it enabled groups suffering from population pressure to find relief through displacement of other groups and thus made it possible for Maori population as a whole to continue to grow without overexploitation and degradation of particular localities. In the remainder of this chapter, we shall see that European influence was disruptive to this process and resulted in new perturbations for the Maoris. And we shall see that it had these effects, not because there was any waning of the traditional motivations, but rather because many of the actions taken on the basis of them had new effects after the introduction of a new technology of warfare and were no longer geared to local population pressures and to variations from group to group in the manpower for defending land and using the available resources.

NEW WEAPONS IN THE SERVICE OF OLD OBJECTIVES

We must speak first about the Maoris' new technology of warfare, and this means speaking, above all, about guns. These were not the only new weapons, for European hatchets, axes, and knives also came to be used in battle. Guns, however, were the most significant introduction. The Maoris began to acquire them in the early years of the nineteenth century, and the first encounters with the weapons filled the people, understandably enough, with fear and awe. This is well indicated in the following account by an English traveler who visited New Zealand in 1814–1815:

> The population of this village was comparatively large, being not less than one hundred and fifty souls, which was a good number for so

inconsiderable a place. It was amusing to see what wild astonishment the
report of a shot produced among the assembled crowd. Firing with my
fowling-piece, at a bird that had settled on an adjacent tree, I happened
to kill it, and this instantly threw the whole village, men, women, and
children into violent confusion; who, knowing not how to account for
the seeming phenomenon, testified the appalling effect it had upon
them, by setting up a tremendous shout, and astounding my ears with
their uproar. While in the act of shewing them the bird I had killed,
which they examined very attentively, perceiving another on the same
tree, I fired at this also, and brought it down; which occasioned a
repetition of their amazement and made them vociferate even louder
than at first. I shewed my shot-bag to one of the old men, but the sight of
it terrified him so much, that he durst not venture to take a second glance
at it; and turning away his head in the greatest trepidation from this
magazine of death, I am persuaded he entertained worse notions of it,
than ever were imagined of Pandora's box (Nicholas, 1817:I, 253–254).

Some of the Maoris, on first seeing guns in operation, attributed
supernatural properties to them and regarded them either as gods
who killed when they "spoke" or as tubes within which thunder and
lightning had been magically confined by the demon Europeans
(White, 1888:V, 172; Best, 1924:II, 286). It did not take long, however,
for some Maoris to acquire a more practical understanding of guns
and the uses to which they could be put. This happened first along
the eastern coasts of the northern part of the North Island, for this
was the area which, initially, received the most frequent calls from
trading and whaling ships. By 1814, when members of the Church
Missionary Society came to the Bay of Islands in this area in order to
establish a station, a local chief, Hongi Hika of the Nga Puhi tribe,
had already been able to teach himself to stock and mount a musket
without any help and he owned several of the weapons (Wright,
1959:86). As we shall see, Hongi's affinity for guns eventually made
him and his people a scourge to other tribes.

The first guns obtained by the Maoris from Europeans were
flintlocks, the type of musket in which a flint in the hammer strikes a
spark, when the trigger is pulled, to ignite the priming. Often the
guns were of poor quality, as European traders had no great scruples
about taking advantage of the Maoris' ignorance of firearms. Moreover, at least at the beginning of the musket era in New Zealand, the
Maoris did not know how to care for the guns and either let them get
wet and unserviceable or else so often took them apart to clean them

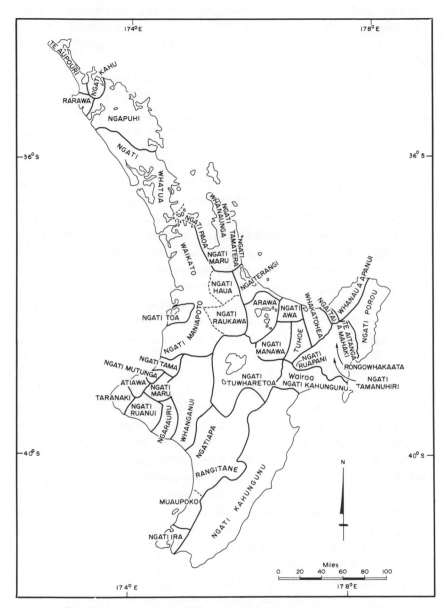

PLATE 13   Maori Tribes in the North Island in 1800

that the locks became loose. According to an English artist who spent nine months in New Zealand in 1827, Maoris were constantly bringing "sick" muskets to Europeans to look at and heal (Earle, 1832:92–93).[9]

Yet, as soon as guns came into use in Maori warfare, they were effective enough. Initially, one or two guns sufficed to give any war party that had them the advantage in fighting against enemies unacquainted with the weapons. This was not so much because of the numbers killed by the guns as because of the panic effected as a result of any killing by them. A good illustration of this is the success of a party of northern warriors who, in 1818, were the first to use guns against the Taranaki peoples of the central western coast of the North Island. The attackers had only two old flintlocks, which they employed to shoot the chiefs of each enemy *pa*. When the defenders heard the noise of the guns and saw their leading warriors fall without, as far as they could see, having been struck, they concluded that supernatural forces were at work—that gods had joined in the fighting. Accordingly, when the attackers stormed a *pa*, they found their enemy panic-stricken and offering no effective resistance to being slaughtered with the traditional Maori clubs and spears. After every battle, the northern war party remained to feast on the flesh of the slain and took care to leave no survivors to carry the alarm to the next settlement (Smith, 1910*a*:286; Walsh, 1907:157).

During this early period, the Maoris calculated the strength of war parties not so much by the number of men they had but rather by the number of muskets. In 1819, a party with 12 muskets was considered strong, while another, armed with 50 guns, was regarded as having terrifying power. As increasing numbers of Maoris learned about the effectiveness of the new weapons, an arms race developed. By 1820, English visitors to the Bay of Islands were estimating that the Maoris there had "some hundred stand of arms" or even as many as 500, and in the following year a Bay of Islands missionary wrote that he did not think there could be "less than two thousand stands of Arms among the Natives" (cited in Wright, 1959:91).[10] By 1826, one of the missionaries was speaking about "many thousand stands of arms." Tribes at some distance from the favored ports of call for European ships were less well supplied, but, once they had suffered from the power of guns, they made the most strenuous efforts to obtain them. The growing overseas demand for such New Zealand products as flax and timber insured a flow of muskets and powder from the Europeans' trading vessels to the Maoris, for the latter increasingly would accept nothing else in exchange for the goods which the foreigners sought. Even the missionaries were sometimes reduced to trading guns to the Maoris in order to obtain food supplies or timber from them. In time, the whole North Island became something like one great camp of musket-armed warriors.

The destructive use of the new means of war in pursuit of the traditional goal of revenge is epitomized in the post-European career of the Nga Puhi chief, Hongi Hika. In 1820, desirous of obtaining arms, he arranged to be taken to England by the missionary, Thomas Kendall. Hongi was presented to King George IV and met a number of other influential persons, who became impressed with his intelligence and his professions of desire to work for the welfare of his people. These professions were not necessarily hypocritical, since, to Hongi's way of thinking, his people's welfare depended upon their acting aggressively to avenge past defeats and injuries. Although he was unsuccessful in obtaining any weapons in England, he did receive numerous gifts of plows and other agricultural tools to help him bring civilization to the Maoris. On the return voyage, Hongi stopped in Sydney and there traded his stock of implements for muskets and powder. These transactions provided him and his people with an armory of 300 guns and a due supply of ammunition.

Less than two months after returning to the Bay of Islands in 1821, Hongi was ready to put the new arms to use. An expedition was organized for revenge against two tribes living to the south, the Ngati Paoa and Ngati Maru of the Hauraki Gulf and Firth of Thames area. A member of the Ngati Paoa tribe had, probably in the previous year, treacherously killed a Nga Puhi man, and the Ngati Maru had defeated Hongi's Nga Puhi in a battle fought with native weapons in the last decade of the eighteenth century. Such murders and defeats called for revenge, and Hongi now had the means of obtaining it. Indeed, he had even declared his purpose in this regard to the Ngati Maru and Ngati Paoa chiefs he had met in Sydney on his return voyage from England. He had displayed his newly acquired arsenal to these enemies and had designated particular guns with the names of past battles which the Nga Puhi had lost and had previously been unable to avenge.

The expedition against the Ngati Paoa and Ngati Maru was of unprecedented magnitude. One of the missionaries, John Butler, observed that when Hongi and his followers set off for the general place of assembly the "whole country for a hundred miles or more" was already on its way to the same place. According to Butler, there had "never been anything like such an arrangement in New Zealand before," and another of the missionaries, Francis Hall, estimated that the expedition was going to have "at least 1000 muskets and perhaps more than double that Number of Men."

The expedition was successful. The relatively few muskets of the people attacked were insufficient to make them any match for the northern forces, and the ramparts and other traditional defenses of the *pa* of Hongi's enemies afforded them little protection when Hongi's men could erect wooden platforms to serve as elevated vantage-points for the firing of musket-balls. In their attacks on only one Ngati Maru *pa* and two Ngati Paoa ones, the Nga Puhi killed some 2,000 people and, according to some accounts, took an equal number as prisoners.

Soon after this expedition, Hongi rallied his followers for another and even more formidable one. According to one missionary observer, there were over 3,000 warriors in the force that embarked from the Bay of Islands at the end of February, 1822. The victims this time were to be the people of the Waikato River, against whom the Nga Puhi had a number of *take*, or causes for war. There was an unavenged Nga Puhi defeat in battle, and there were also some specific deaths for which the Waikato were held responsible, especially the deaths of two young chiefs who had been killed in the previous year as they were attacking the Ngati Maru *pa*, which some Waikato were helping to defend.

On hearing about the new Nga Puhi expedition, the Waikato people, who had no guns, assembled in a single, very large *pa*, perhaps in the hope that their numbers alone (variously estimated at between 5,000 and 10,000 people) might save them. This was not to be the case. Indeed, the issue was decided almost immediately after Hongi's warriors arrived at the *pa* and disembarked from their canoes. The guns were fired, and the people inside the *pa*, many of whom had not previously seen the European weapons in operation, began to flee in dread. As the firing increased, so did the panic of those inside. Many of the fleeing fell into the ditch surrounding the *pa*, and the first to fall had others fall on top of them with the result that some hundreds were smothered or trodden to death. The Waikato warriors who waited to meet the attackers in close combat were shot as they rushed up to enemy fighters in order to be near enough to them for the use of wooden weapons. The Waikato were driven from the *pa* and suffered, by the estimate which Hongi subsequently gave to the missionaries, the loss of 1,500 people. Nga Puhi deaths in the engagement were but a small fraction of this.

Before Hongi's death in 1828, he and other Nga Puhi chiefs led campaigns against tribes of various other districts, including Kaipara, which is near to the Bay of Islands, and the Bay of Plenty and the East Coast, which are far away, farther than any Nga Puhi war parties had ranged prior to the nineteenth century.[11] The objective in these campaigns, which resulted in the slaughter of several thousand more Maoris, still was vengeance. Thus, the major Nga Puhi expedition in 1823, against a Bay of Plenty tribe called Te Arawa, was in revenge for a Te Arawa subtribe's treacherous massacre of a Nga Puhi party in 1822. And Hongi's last great victory, against the Ngati Whatua of Kaipara in 1825, was the Nga Puhi's revenge for a series of stinging defeats in pre-musket times, particularly a defeat in which 150 or more Nga Puhi had died at Moremo-nui stream in 1807. Hongi's father and half-brother were among those who had fallen in battle at Moremo-nui, and his sister had also been killed there by some Ngati Whatua, who, before Hongi's eyes, had first subjected her body to various abuses and had then thrown her alive onto the hot oven stones. It is said that Hongi's main purpose in making his trip to England had been to secure arms for avenging the deaths at Moremo-nui.

Their expeditions earned Hongi and the Nga Puhi an early notoriety, but there were others, like the Ngati Toa led by Te Rauparaha and the Ngati Haua led by Te Waharoa, who also raided widely, frequently, and fiercely once they got hold of muskets. Te Rauparaha and his men even carried the new brand of warfare across Cook Strait to the east coast of the South Island, where they raided as far south as Kaiapoi near the present city of Christchurch. In the North Island, there was hardly any district spared from the depredations of warriors armed with guns.

These other aggressors of the musket era were also, for the most part, bent upon revenge. Acquisition of guns enabled them to square accounts with numerous traditional enemies at whose hands they had suffered defeats in earlier warfare with native weapons. And, it should be noted, such traditional enemies were not the only ones against whom guns were directed by revenge-seekers in the 1820s and 1830s. Any injuries received from friends and allies of an attacked foe had also to be avenged and now for the first time, with guns available, readily could be. This is illustrated by the fact that in Hongi's defeat of the Waikato, he was, as previously noted, obtaining revenge for the Nga Puhi deaths inflicted by Waikato warriors in the course of their defense of the Ngati Maru *pa* less than a year earlier. Te Rauparaha's first attack upon the Ngai Tahu of the South Island was similarly motivated by a desire for revenge, for some Ngai Tahu had participated in an unsuccessful attack upon Te Rauparaha's forces on Kapiti Island near the present city of Wellington and one of their chiefs was known to have subsequently uttered the insulting boast that "if ever Te Rauparaha dared to set foot on his land, he would rip his belly open with a shark's tooth" (Buick, 1911:122).

In the case of Te Rauparaha's wars, there was fighting for land as well as fighting for revenge. Some writers have interpreted territorial conquests by Te Rauparaha and other Maoris in the musket era as evidence of certain new motivations for war—motivations which we might, for convenience, call "Napoleonic," since they are alleged to have been patterned on the example of Napoleon's career of empire-building in Europe. (For examples of this interpretation, see Smith, 1910b:15 and the citations in Wright, 1959:119–121) The interpretation cannot be said to be well founded, for, regardless of the knowledge that particular chiefs may have had of Napoleon's career, it remains a fact that the conquests of the 1820s and 1830s were cast

PLATE 14   War Speech by Maori Chief, 1827

much more in the traditional Maori mold than in any Napoleonic one. Specifically, there is no evidence of effective political consolidation as a result or even as an aim of the conquests. Defeated people were not as a rule kept on their former land and there made politically subject to their conquerors. Instead, following the traditional pattern, conquerors endeavored for the most part to kill members of the defeated group and to exclude them from their former territories. Te Rauparaha, designated by one biographer as the "Napoleon of the South," does not seem to have been an exception to this. He is described by the same biographer (Buick, 1911:87) as having preached to his followers a doctrine of exterminating the North Island tribes whose lands in the Wellington vicinity the Ngati Toa were taking.[12]

In the case of the campaigns led by Hongi, there were never even any attempts to take over the lands of defeated enemies. And this was the chief whom the missionary, Samuel Marsden (1932:386, 388), had proposed as the person to become a king and bring peace and a stable government to New Zealand. The fact is that Hongi was never fully successful in securing his authority even within his own tribe. As long as he was well supplied with guns and other Nga Puhi chiefs were not, he could call out all the sections of the tribe for his expeditions, for none wished to have Hongi's guns directed against themselves. Even so, in the attack on one of the Ngati Paoa *pa* in the expedition of 1821, the men of four or five of the Nga Puhi subtribes asserted their independence by refusing to take part, although they did join their tribesmen in the remainder of the campaign. And the bullet wound from which Hongi eventually died was received in a battle in which some of his former followers were arrayed against him. Later, when guns were general among the Maoris, the war-cry could, according to one missionary, go from village to village in the Bay of Islands without any effect and it was with the "utmost difficulty" that a sufficient number of men could be mobilized to take part in fighting beyond their own immediate districts (Yate, 1835:119).[13] There was no fuel here for Napoleonic ambitions. The reasonable interpretation is the one suggested earlier: that new means were being used in the service of traditional objectives.

A DISRUPTED PROCESS

It remains to draw together the evidence on how the use of the new means, together with certain other features of Maori intercourse with Europeans, disrupted the traditional process previously described and, furthermore, resulted in new perturbations for the Maoris.

It must be noted first that Maori warfare, like Iban headhunting in the late eighteenth or early nineteenth century, became less localized. Revenge-seeking Maoris of the musket era were turning their guns not only upon the nearby enemies with whom the traditional process could operate in pre-European times through repeated raids and counter-raids and regulated escalations to attempted territorial conquests. Expeditions now were undertaken to distant places in retaliation for offenses. Some of these offenses could not even have been committed if not for Maori intercourse with Europeans. Examples of this are the offenses that developed when European ships landed Maoris in parts of New Zealand far from their homes. Among the people thus put ashore were stowaways, temporary seamen that could not be taken back to England, men intended for labor in timber cutting, and even women sold as slaves. Conflicts inevitably developed between some of these Maoris and the local inhabitants and resulted in insults and injuries which constituted intertribal offenses involving tribes that had had virtually no intercourse with one another previously. Among the more notorious illustrations of this are the fates of the women abducted in 1806 from various points in the northern part of the North Island by a crew of European mutineers on the brig *Venus*. The women were eventually sold by the sailors to chiefs in the Bay of Plenty and East Coast districts and served for a time as wives and slaves there and then, when quarrels arose, were put to death. It was in revenge for these offenses that some of the earliest Nga Puhi expeditions against distant tribes took place.[14]

Other expeditions beyond the pre-European range of military operations resulted from the fact that any injuries received by an attacking force from friends and allies of the enemy could now, with

guns available, also be readily avenged. Hongi's expedition against
the Waikato people in 1822 illustrates this, since he was, as previously noted, obtaining revenge for the Nga Puhi deaths inflicted by
Waikato warriors in the course of their defense of a Ngati Maru *pa* in
1821. Te Rauparaha's first expedition across Cook Strait against the
Ngai Tahu of the South Island was, it should be recalled, similarly
motivated.

Such expeditions against faraway tribes could not be undertaken
before the nineteenth century. While there were no guns to give
security to attacking parties, distant places were full of peril for them
because any people attacked there would have many friends and
allies nearby. In making the distant expeditions possible for some
Maoris, the guns also spread the reliance on guns: groups that had
suffered from or were threatened by the muskets of enemies set
about to get their own. There was no parallel to this among the Ibans
in the period of their headhunting in the Borneo coastal areas, and
the greater disruption of the traditional war process among the
Maoris than among the Ibans in the nineteenth century may be
attributed largely to the effects of the arms races that developed
among the Maoris throughout the North Island of New Zealand.
These arms races, as will be indicated below, were expensive in men
and resources for the Maoris. And all combatants in all phases of
fighting had to have guns, for, if one side were not to use them, the
other surely would. In other words, costliness in resources and lives
became an attribute of all warfare among the Maoris rather than of
just the later phases of a multiphase war process.

What made the arms races costly? There was, first of all, widespread neglect of subsistence labors as all Maoris applied themselves
to the tasks of producing the flax and other goods that could be
traded to Europeans for guns and ammunition.[15] One European
observer, F. E. Maning (1876:162–163), who lived with the Maoris
from 1833 on, noted that for one or two muskets the people had to
give a ton of flax, "scraped by hand with a shell, bit by bit, morsel by
morsel, half-quarter of an ounce at a time." Maning's conclusion was
the following:

> Now as the natives, when undisturbed and labouring regularly at their
> cultivations, were never far removed from necessity or scarcity of food,

PLATE 15 Maori War-Dance in the Musket Era

we may easily imagine the distress and hardship caused by this enor-
mous imposition of extra labour. They were obliged to neglect their crops
in a very serious degree, and for many months in the year were in a half-
starving condition, working hard all the time in the flax swamps.

As Maning's statement suggests, the Maoris, because of the
arms races, not only were neglecting their subsistence labors but also
were working themselves to exhaustion in producing goods for
trade. And the need for guns had yet another effect which made the
Maoris easy prey for disease—especially pulmonary disease—and
death. This was the move from airy villages on high ground to
makeshift residences by the swamps where the flax grew best. Being
situated on hilltops, to which food, fuel, and water had to be carried
from below, had been an advantage for defense against attacking
parties in the days of the native weapons but was no longer so.
Moreover, time, made newly precious by having to work in order to
get guns, could now be saved by the Maoris by living nearer to the
flax and timber and also to what sources of provisions for themselves
were available. And so the people descended to the lowlands and
there, as was noted by Maning (1876:160) among others:

> In mere swamps they built their oven-like houses, where the water even
> in summer sprung with the pressure of the foot, and where in winter the
> houses were often completely flooded. There, lying on the spongy soil,
> on beds of rushes which rotted under them—in little, low dens of
> houses, or kennels, heated like ovens at night and dripping with damp
> in the day . . . and impossible to ventilate—they were cut off by disease
> in a manner absolutely frightful.

Increase in the mortality in actual warfare contributed to the
disruption of the traditional war process. The Nga Puhi, it will be
recalled, are said to have killed some 3,500 people in only their first
two expeditions after Hongi's return from England. This estimate
may be exaggerated to some extent, but it is probably safe to assume
that the people slaughtered in the course of Hongi's several expeditions in the musket era did number in the thousands. In the later
fights or battles in which both sides were well armed with guns, the
number of casualties relative to the number of combatants may often
have been less than in the old days of hand-to-hand fighting when
many men could be killed once a rout had commenced, but any
declines in mortality in actual warfare in the latter part of the musket

era may have been offset by the deaths from starvation and disease resulting from the arms races.[16]

Accurate figures on the number of Maoris that perished in one way or another because of the muskets in the early nineteenth century are unavailable. However, nobody seems to have estimated the number at less than 20,000 and some have reckoned it as high as 80,000 and have suggested that between one quarter and one half of the total number of Maoris in New Zealand was lost.[17] Even if we allow for substantial exaggeration in the last estimates referred to, we can still be sure that the Maori losses on account of the guns were very considerable.

It can be seen that even if the Maori warfare of the musket era was, as previously noted, similar in some respects to either some recent Maring warfare or to the extensive coastal headhunting by the Ibans, it was only among the Maoris that costliness in resources and lives became an attribute of all warfare rather than of just the later phases of a multiphase war process. In the Iban case, even when the establishment of fortified downriver outstations by the English finally made extensive headhunting in the coastal areas too costly, the Ibans could still revert to localized hostilities operating as part of a multiphase process in Borneo's interior. And, among the Marings, in the absence of conditions conducive to escalation to territorial conquests, the hostilities that continued to occur were appropriate to the prevailing demographic and ecological conditions and in keeping with the traditional functioning of the Maring multiphase war process. It was only in the Maori case that all fighting everywhere had become costly. By using new weapons in the service of old objectives, the Maoris were in effect producing new perturbations for themselves. These were perturbations to which there could be no adequate responses so long as the Maoris held on to their ideas about the necessity of taking revenge.

Actually the lag in the development of new responses was not very long. The magnitude of the perturbations was great enough to affect even deeply ingrained ideas and behavior. By 1830, the value of fighting for revenge was, according to the missionaries' accounts, being questioned by many of the Nga Puhi, who found themselves increasingly beset by death and illness and threatened by their erstwhile victims who now also had guns (see the citations in Wright, 1959:100, 147). Moreover, when all the tribes were equipped with muskets, it soon became apparent that easy victories could no longer be won. Many Maoris turned to Christianity for a new set of values whereby not taking revenge for injuries suffered could, most opportunely, be justified. In the late 1830s and early 1840s, conversion to Christianity was rapid and massive, and firearms were cast aside.[18] The war process, which had operated adaptively in pre-European times but now seemed to produce only death, destruction, and despair, was abandoned.

EPILOGUE

The conversions to Christianity did not make the Maoris men of peace forever. They took up arms again years later to prevent their lands from being taken by the European settlers who had been coming to New Zealand in increasing numbers from 1840 on.[19] Although this new fighting was not a reversion to the disrupted, traditional Maori war process, the recourse to firearms when the Maoris' lands were in jeopardy may be regarded as a return to responses which, unlike much of the fighting for revenge in the pre-1840 musket era, were appropriate in magnitude to the magnitude of the perturbations.

5

SUMMARY

In the case studies of the preceding chapters, war has been viewed, not simply as something that either does or does not occur, but rather as a process with distinguishable phases. This has made it possible for us to see that escalations from phase to phase in war processes are not inevitable; that the causes of entry into war may be different from the causes of moving from one phase to another; that, in cases of escalation to territorial conquests, war processes can be effective in counteracting stresses associated with population pressure; and that the multiphase character of the processes can help to keep the later phases, which are expensive in resources and lives, from occurring prematurely.

A major concern of the preceding chapters has been the conditions under which processes persist and those under which they break down. Both the Maring and Iban cases illustrate the persistence of war processes that can escalate to territorial conquests. We have seen from these cases that such persistence need not end because of long periods without territorial conquests or because of periods during which hostilities are undertaken (as they were by the Ibans) against groups living too far away for territorial conquests from them to be feasible as the result of an escalating process.

The one war process shown not to have persisted was that of the Maoris of New Zealand. This had formerly been like what the Marings and Ibans continued to have: a multiphase process that operated at times to counteract perturbations and did not deprive people of adequate resources for dealing with further stresses. But after the Maoris adopted muskets in fighting, costliness in resources and lives became an attribute of all Maori warfare rather than of just the later phases of a multiphase process; the war process itself became a major source of stresses for the people. As such, it was abandoned after about two decades of deadly hostilities with the muskets, notwithstanding that the behavior involved in the process was based on deeply ingrained (or "hard-programmed") ideas that the Maoris held about revenge. Evidently even such processes may be eliminated when perturbations attain sufficient magnitudes. A more general way of stating this is that the persistence or nonpersistence of processes that interfere with responses to perturbations—or somehow themselves become the source of them—depends, *inter alia*, on the magnitudes that perturbations attain.

It can be seen from this summary, as well as from the book as a whole, that subject matters such as war and population pressure may be analyzable in terms of variables appropriate to consider in other analyses of perturbations and the processes responding to them. Among these variables are the magnitude, duration, and frequency of perturbations, the magnitude and reversibility of responses to them, the temporal order in which responses of different magnitudes occur, and the persistence or nonpersistence of response processes. These, in fact, are the kinds of variables that must be dealt with in order to develop further and to test some potentially important generalizations that have already been put forward by social scientists or human ecologists whose primary focus has been on neither population pressure nor war processes. Among examples are statements to the effect that selection favors structures using "expensive" control mechanisms only when they are needed—a "principle" that Stinchcombe, in a sociological discussion, illustrates by citing the infrequent recourse to political purges in societies (Stinchcombe, 1968:145–146). There also are similar but broader generalizations about how the adaptedness of living systems depends on maintaining a general homeostasis that derives from a certain ordering of processes (Rappaport, 1974; cf. Slobodkin, 1974:69; Slobodkin and Rapoport, 1974:196–199). It should become possible to develop further such generalizations about adaptedness and adaptive responses and to make testable predictions on the basis of them as the discrimination of the response processes operating in complex systems and the enumeration and quantification of relevant variables proceed. All of this is work to which the analysis of war processes in an ecological perspective can contribute.

NOTES

CHAPTER 1

1. The disagreements here may remain difficult to resolve empirically for some time to come, partly because of the grave inadequacies of our tools and techniques for ascertaining carrying capacities (see Street, 1969).
2. It may be of interest to note that there may be cases in which the ultimate phase of a war process results in solutions to problems, not of population pressure, but of population shortage—as perhaps among the Marind-Anim of the southern coast of West New Guinea, a people whose elaborate rituals culminated sometimes in headhunting expeditions to distant places where children were captured for adoption (van Baal, 1966). Some critics of my New Guinea case study have misconstrued my objectives insofar as they have assumed that the study was a part of a program designed to show the preeminence or universality of certain environmental or ecological causes of warfare (Hallpike, 1973; Koch, 1974:Chap. 7).
3. Arguments supporting a similar enterprise in biology are presented by Slobodkin and Rapoport (1974). Slobodkin's ideas, as presented in his published papers and various personal communications, have had a considerable influence on my own. It should be noted, however, that I am more optimistic than he about the applicability of these ideas to the analysis of human responses to perturbations. In his view, the "human tendency to develop a normative introspective self image"

results in "deviations from the pattern of evolutionary strategy found in most animals" (Slobodkin, MS).

CHAPTER 2

1. Linguists have classified the Maring language as belonging to the Central Family in the Eastern New Guinea Highlands stock (Wurm and Laycock, 1961; Bunn and Scott, 1963).
2. The imprecision in my statement of the number and size of the clan cluster populations in the more densely settled parts of the Maring area is mainly a result of my being uncertain whether some of the groups whose densities could not be estimated (because usable air photographs of their territories had not been made) are to be regarded as being in the more densely settled parts or not. As discussed in Lowman-Vayda (1968:202–203 and Note 4 on p. 240), it was possible to make estimates of densities in the territories in which almost half of the total Maring population resides.
3. Before being fully aware of the importance of the differences between the more densely and less densely settled groups, I myself described *all* Marings as belonging to clan cluster populations (Vayda and Cook, 1964). For examples of the broad definitions that permit this usage, see Clarke, 1971:27; Lowman-Vayda, 1968:205. Contrasts similar to those between the more and less densely settled Maring groups have been observed by Meggitt (1957b:37 ff.; 1965:272) between the Ipili and Mae Enga peoples of New Guinea's central highlands.
4. This sequence has been described in detail by Rappaport (1967) from the vantage point of the Tsembaga clan cluster.
5. Similar distributions of territories have been reported both from other parts of the world and from elsewhere in New Guinea (Brookfield and Brown, 1963:170).
6. Conducted by Roy and Ann Rappaport, Cherry Lowman, and myself under a National Science Foundation grant (No. G23173).
7. The cases of territorial encroachment are referred to in the final section of this chapter.
8. On the Maori practice in this regard, see Vayda, 1960:45.
9. This is a view presented in detail by Rappaport in his book (1967) on Maring ritual and ecology; he also notes (p. 152, note) that there have been violations of the ritual proscriptions. Three cases of what may have been violations are known to me: the Kauwatyi raid on the Tyenda in 1955, the fighting initiated by the Manamban against the Kauwatyi in 1956, and the Tukumenga attack on the Manamban in 1956. Details of these hostilities are given elsewhere in this chapter.
10. The figures are based on the pigs and people involved in the festival held by the Tsembaga clan cluster population in 1962–63, as described by Rappaport (1967). Groups smaller than the Tsembaga and with smaller territories held festivals with considerably fewer pigs, while larger groups are said to have held festivals with several hundred pigs. Elsewhere (Vayda, 1972:907) I have made the following observations: " . . . the people tend to hold the festivals when they can afford to— when they have had good fortune for a number of years and when, accordingly,

pigs may have become 'too much of a good thing' for them. Indeed, there is evidence that when pig herds become large they also become burdensome and cause people to agitate for inception of the pig festivals, for expanding pig populations increasingly compete with human beings for garden food and their care calls for larger and larger outlays of energy" (cf. Rappaport, 1967:153–165; Vayda, Leeds, and Smith, 1961). One Simbai valley group, the Kanumb–Manekai, with a resident population of 91 , was beginning its festival in March 1963, and informants from the group told me that they had originally planned to wait for the return of some of their young men from coastal employment before holding their festival but then had had to decide to go ahead without them—because there were "too many pigs destroying gardens." When I made a census of Kanumb–Manekai pigs in June 1963 (prior to the wholesale killing of pigs in connection with the festival), I found 62 adult pigs (23 males and 39 females) and 26 piglets.

11. The most recent war in which a main belligerent was the Tsembaga clan cluster studied by Rappaport (1967:218) began within three months of the end of a Tsembaga pig festival. In the case of the last war between the Yomban and Manga clusters of the Jimi Valley, the first provocation to fight was made while the Yomban were still engaged in their pig festival. Their old enemies, the Manga, shouted at them as follows: "You're not men—you're women. We killed some of you, but you didn't kill us. So what are you making a festival for?" The incensed Yomban concluded their festival and then quickly repaired to Manga territory where they killed one Manga man and four women in a garden by first spearing them and then cutting them up with axes. The war was on.

12. This comparison is based on Clarke, 1966:348–352. Further discussion of differential pressure on the land is presented in the concluding section of this chapter.

13. For descriptions of Maring shields and their use, see Lowman, 1973.

14. There are illustrations of both kinds of decisions in Maring informants' accounts of warfare—for example, fights between the Irimban and Yomban clusters and between the Manamban and Tukumenga clusters.

15. A description of these preparations is given in Rappaport, 1967:125–138.

16. The exception consisted of a war in which the Tukumenga stayed on the north bank of the wide and deep Jimi River and their adversaries, the Mima, stayed on the south bank. Actual fighting was limited to shooting arrows across the water. After more than a month of this and with nobody killed, some Tukumenga said, "It is no good to fight distant enemies. Our bellies are still angry; so let us kill some people nearby." They found two Manamban men doing garden work and killed them. The Tukumenga then abandoned the war against the Mima and fought the Manamban (cf. Vayda, 1967:134).

17. The Yomban are the easternmost Maring group in the Jimi Valley. The Manga are the next group to the east and are Narak-speakers but have customs in warfare hardly different from those of their Maring neighbors (see Cook, 1967). Adopting the terminology favored by some anthropologists (e.g., Salisbury, 1963:257–258), we could say that the Yomban and the Manga belong to a single "league."

18. Including those described in Rappaport, 1967:152, Note 9, citing accounts that I obtained in 1966 from Tukumenga participants in the the fighting.

19. My account of the aftermath of the routing of the Manga is based upon information both from Yomban informants and from written résumés of the official patrol

reports. The résumés were kindly supplied to me in 1963 by Mr. J. K. McCarthy, then director of the Department of Native Affairs, Territory of Papua and New Guinea. Other reports of government contacts with Maring groups, including the reports on which the next four paragraphs in this section of the present chapter are based, were kindly made available to me by the Simbai and Tabibuga patrol officers in 1963 and 1966. Published accounts of the Patrol Post at Tabibuga and some of the work done from there include Attenborough, 1960:Chapter 5, and Souter, 1964:235.

20. See the final section of this chapter.

21. The Manamban and the Manga in the Jimi Valley and the Kono and the Angoiang in the Simbai Valley have done this. After the Australian officer and his policemen had demonstrated the power of their magic by shooting six Yomban dead, some of the Yomban went to hunting grounds that they had north of the crest of the Bismarck Range and they made settlements there.

22. Rappaport (1967:166 ff.) gives details of the stake-planting ceremonies.

23. Here, as before, I am defining as "more densely settled" those groups that have either close to 100 people or many more per square mile of land under cultivation or in secondary forest. Tyenda density prior to the land transfers was only about 60 people per square mile of such land.

24. What if a group suffering from population pressure finds itself, sooner or later, in deadlock with every group whose power it tests in warfare? This is a hypothetical situation on which we have no evidence from the Marings. Nevertheless, we can speculate that when relief from population pressure is unobtainable through the operation of the war process or some other behavioral processes, it is likely to be provided through the operation of various physiological processes which limit population by leading to lowered resistance to disease and death, lowered fertility, and lowered viability of offspring.

25. It should be noted that with regard to PF used as hunting grounds by Marings there was not always clear definition of what was within a group's territorial boundaries and what was not. I plan to devote an article to a consideration of the significance of the varying nature of rights to hunting grounds among the Marings. Here, for the purpose of calculating the size of group territories and the extent of PF within them, I have followed two somewhat arbitrary rules: (1) to regard as being within a group's territory all of the forest which the members of *only* that group described as being theirs; and (2) to regard as not belonging to any group those portions of the forest to which members of more than one autonomous group claimed rights.

26. Some of the groups that were converting portions of their PF into farmed land after warfare are specified in Note 21. A constraint that should be noted here is that almost all groups had some PF located on land too high (and therefore too cold or too often covered by clouds) for effective cultivation of root crops by Maring techniques.

27. PF resources utilized by the Marings are included in the lists provided in Clarke, 1971:Appendices B and D, and Rappaport, 1967:Appendix 8.

28. This was first suggested to me by Cherry Lowman.

29. Population density of the 55,000 Central Enga "averages about 110 to 120 per square mile" and some Enga groups have densities of over 300 people per square

mile (Meggitt, 1962:158; 1972:113). Density in the Maring region as a whole averages less than 50 people per square mile and no Maring group has a density exceeding an average of 85 per square mile of a group's total territory. For contrasts in intensity of land use between Maring areas and a location in the Tairora-speaking region of the eastern part of the highlands, see Clarke (1966). Also, see Brookfield's table (1962:244–245) presenting data on 25 highland localities.

30. For example, the Chimbu as described by Brookfield and Brown (1963:79) and by Vial (1942:especially p. 8).

31. On the definition of adaptive responses, see Chapter 3, Note 16.

CHAPTER 3

1. We will not be concerned here with details of the Ibans' treatment of heads. For a vivid description see Horsburgh, 1858:28–33. A section on "Methods of Decapitation and Preservation" is included in the chapter on headhunting in Roth (1896:II,145–156).

2. We are assuming 25 years per generation. As the historian Pringle (1970:39) notes, this seems reasonable in light of modern Iban marriage practice.

3. Cf. Fürer-Haimendorf's observations, made in a discussion of the morality of headhunting among the Nagas of Assam: " . . . once a society accepts that the presence of captured heads in a village magically benefits the whole community, it is logical that great social prestige and merit should be gained by the successful head-hunter. The meritoriousness of his deed . . . . lies in the concrete achievement of adding human heads, and with them life-giving force, to the village" (Fürer-Haimendorf, 1967:100–101).

4. Tarling (1963:6–11) summarizes the influence that Dutch policies had upon piracy. See also Crawfurd, 1820:III, 233 ff.; Logan, 1847:17; Raffles, 1921:vii–ix; Sopher, 1965:255.

5. When Rentap, a famous leader of the Skrang Ibans, was asked in the 1840s why he was fond of attacking different places, his answer was: "Because I am fond of heads." He took plunder also (gold, silver, and "other things"), but the cause he gave for his expeditions was the desire for heads (Abdulkassim's testimony in Reports, 1855:181).

6. One coastal trader told of having heard that Ibans had attacked even further north than Mukah, i.e., as far as Bintulu in the Fourth Division (Abdullrahim's testimony in Reports, 1855:197). Nevertheless, while the distance along the coast between Pontianak and either Mukah or Bintulu does amount to several hundred miles, Keppel's statement (1853:I, 129) that Iban fleets ranged over a distance of 800 miles must be reckoned an exaggeration.

7. In a paper submitted to the commissioners in Singapore in 1854, Rajah Brooke first cited a Saribas man's deposition about participation in attacks on numerous Chinese towns in the Dutch territories and then asked whether there is then an "intertribal war between Holland and Serebas [Saribas]" (Reports, 1855:271; for the Saribas man's deposition, see Keppel, 1853:II, 269–270).

8. This changed in the 1850s as Rajah Brooke's officers, especially Charles Brooke who later became the second white rajah, developed the policy of using "pacified" downriver Skrang and Saribas Ibans on expeditions against upriver ones (see below and Pringle, 1970:92, 103–104, 107–109, 128–129).

9. For details of developments described sketchily in this paragraph, see Irwin (1955:Chaps. 1–4); Runciman (1960:Chap. 2); Tarling (1963:Introduction and Chap. 3). On the absence of "any meaningful central Government" specifically in Sarawak's Second Division during the first period of Iban aggressions along the coast, see Pringle (1970:44).

10. This was another of Commissioner Devereux's conclusions. For the testimony on which it was based, see *Reports* (1855:32–33 and *passim*). When one Malay witness, the Dato Patinggi of Sarawak, was asked whether the Saribas and Skrang Ibans preferred the heads of the Land Dayaks and other Ibans to those of the Malays or Chinese of Sarawak, his answer was: "All skulls are alike to them, there is no choice" (*Reports*, 1855:135).

11. There was no parallel to this among nineteenth century Maoris, whose commitment to revenge-seeking imposed a restriction on the range of possible victims of attacks. If we want a parallel to the nature of Iban headhunting in the early nineteenth century, we can find it in some robberies in American cities in the 1970s as reported, for example, in the following three paragraphs from an article in the *New York Times Magazine* on "The 'Rat Packs' of New York":

> The old gangs and groups, for all their murderous fury, fought mostly among themselves. While race (or nationality) was often involved, it was a *de facto* racism brought about by the neighborhood boundaries. The struggle was localized and though money was often an issue, it was "revolving" money, neighborhood money stolen or extorted and kept in local circulation.
>
> By the start of the seventies, the country's racial rupture and economic inequalities had filtered through to consciousness in the minds of the youthful poor . . . .The depressed economy meant even less money in the slums, and the young, as always, were the first to feel the crunch. Spending money had to be got from outside, and so the whole city became the arena. Rip offs were to be done anywhere, to anybody— preferably to a member of another race, religion, nationality or culture, but basically anyone with money. Violence became an accident of time and place.
>
> The phenomenon is now seemingly endemic to large cities. In New York, as might be expected, it involves predominantly those youths who have the least opportunity and the most grievances—largely, but far from exclusively, black and Spanish-speaking residents. While the gangs and groups of the past fed on their own, today's rat packs, formed along racial lines—all white or Puerto Rican or black—feed on everybody else. For them, the city is one big cheese wheel (Stevens, 1971:91; © 1971 by The New York Times Company; reprinted by permission).

12. These remarks by Charles Brooke are cited also in Pringle's Chap. 2 (1970); on which my picture of the relations between Malay chiefs and Iban headhunters is based. On the relations between Brunei and the local Malay chiefs in Sarawak, see also Irwin (1955:73) and Brown (1970:Chaps. 8, 9, and 11).

13. Low, who originally came to Sarawak as a botanist in 1845, stated that he

conversed frequently with the Ibans about headhunting and that they "merely accounted for it, in their usual method, by saying, that it was the adat ninik, or custom of their ancestors" (Low, 1848:188–189).

14. As Pringle notes, St. John and Rajah Brooke questioned this figure and argued that the number killed in the battle itself was 300 and that 500 more died later, either walking home through the jungle or at the hands of Ibans allied with the rajah (Pringle, 1970:83, citing *Reports* 1855:203 and Templer 1853:II, 282, 284). For details of the British expeditions of the 1840s, Pringle (1970: Chap. 3) should be consulted. His account is much clearer than that of earlier historians, who accepted "piracy" as a suitable characterization of Saribas and Skrang activities.

15. For a fuller account of the attack on Skrang Fort, see Baring-Gould and Bampfylde (1909:155–157). Rentap, to whom we have previously referred, was the leader of the attack, and one of Brooke's officers, Alan Lee, died in the course of it.

16. Adaptive responses are those which contribute positively to adaptedness, and I regard adaptedness, like health, as being definable for individuals and populations in terms of their ability to deal with—and survive—not only the stresses or perturbations currently occurring but also those likely to occur in the near future (cf. Audy 1971; Montgomery 1973; Sargent 1966; Scudder 1973; Slobodkin 1968; Slobodkin and Rapoport 1974).

17. On the new alignments in Iban hostilities, see below and Pringle (1970:92 ff).

18. Charles Brooke estimated in 1915 that he himself had commanded about 50 of these expeditions (cited in Pringle, 1970:322). In other times and places, indigenes had been used militarily against other indigenes by poor and weak foreign governments attempting to extend their sway (see Gibson, 1952:22–27 and Powell, 1952:Chap. 9 for examples from sixteenth-century Mexico), but not surprisingly the Sarawak Government's use of headhunters in particular resulted in criticism of the second white rajah's methods of spreading civilization (Pringle, 1970:240–245, 357–359).

19. In Freeman's view, some of the deleterious ways of using land are and have long been "an essential feature of the Iban system of shifting cultivation" and have gone "hand in hand with the remarkable advance of the Iban into the Rejang basin and beyond" (Freeman, 1970:286). I do not regard Freeman's view to imply that the methods in question were commonly employed prior to the Great Kayan Expedition. Unfortunately, evidence on the antiquity of the methods as prevalent ones is unavailable.

20. That processes similar to the one described in the present chapter were operating among the Nagas is suggested by the fact that some of the Naga tribes—for example, the Konyak (Fürer-Haimendorf, 1969:54, 95)—are reported to have fought "normally" for heads and not for land and yet at times to have taken land. The Nagas in general, like the Ibans, believed in the magical power of heads and, as noted by Hutton (1921:160 ff.; 1928:403 ff.), undertook headhunting expeditions in response to misfortunes.

CHAPTER 4

1. This and the succeeding three paragraphs on expansion among the Maoris and the Tiv are taken, with some changes, from Vayda, 1961a:348–350.

2. The conquest of the Auckland isthmus, described in this chapter, occurred during what Buck regards as a period of stabilized land when wars were not fought for territory.

3. This and the succeeding paragraph on retaliation are based on Vayda, 1960:43–45.

4. Revenge as a Maori value has often been discussed. See, for example, Best, 1924:II, 232; Buck, 1949:388; Busby, 1832:62; Carleton, 1948:178; Cook, 1967:71; Gudgeon, 1904:258–260; Johansen, 1954:61–83; Shortland, 1856:230; Smith, 1896–97:72; Smith, 1910b:329–330.

5. For descriptions of Maori councils of war, see Buck (1949:389); Savage (1939:35, 37); White (1874:Chap. 2).

6. On conquerors' rights and related aspects of Maori land tenure, see Acheson (1931); Firth (1959:Chap. 11); Smith (1942); White (1885:183–216).

7. An early nineteenth-century example of attempted reconquest by people who had been in refuge is described in Kelly (1949:297–298).

8. For more detailed accounts of the conquest of the Auckland isthmus, see Smith (1896–97:83–91); Kelly (1949:253–257).

9. A discussion similar to mine in this and the succeeding paragraph has been presented by Wright (1959:84–85). (Cf. Travers, 1872:46–47.)

10. Chapter 5 of Wright's book (1959) is a valuable secondary source on the introduction and spread of muskets among the Maoris. Other sources that I have used in writing the paragraphs on the use of muskets in Maori warfare are Binney, 1968:85 ff.; Gudgeon, 1885:Chaps. 11, 13–21; Hall, 1823; Hamlin, 1842:345–354; Lesson, 1839:II, Chap. 21; Smith, 1910b:15–18 and passim; Tapp, 1958:Chap. 3 and p. 178; Thomson, 1859:I, 258–262, 298–299; Travers, 1872:47; Urlich, 1970; Walsh, 1907:157f.; White, 1888:–V, 168–176. The quotation on p. 92 from the journal of the Rev. John Butler is taken from Wright (1959:92). My account of the offenses that Hongi Hika of the Nga Puhi was avenging in his expeditions is based mainly on Smith 1910b:46–49, 177–179, 182–184, 198, 204–207, 225, 241–242, and 330 (cf. Kelly, 1938:179–180; Marsden, 1932:242–243).

11. According to the traditional accounts, the Hauraki Gulf was the furthest south that any expedition of northern warriors penetrated until the early years of the nineteenth century (Smith, 1910b:17; cf. Firth, 1929:430).

12. Buick (1911:126) suggests that Te Rauparaha may have pursued a different policy in the South Island, but the details are hazy.

13. Other sources on the question of Hongi's authority are Marsden (1932:388); Smith (1910b:189, 398); Vayda (1960:33); White (1885:222–223); Wright (1959:120–121).

14. My discussion of Maoris put ashore away from their homes follows Wright (1959:83–84). On the abductions by the Venus crew, see also Smith (1910b:56–57, 90, 156) and the references cited in Vennell (1967:179).

15. Production for trade rather than for Maori subsistence is also the work to which were assigned the large numbers of slaves being kept for the first time by some tribes. That the free people often worked harder and longer than did the slaves did not matter as long as the slaves' work, like the free people's, resulted in an increment to the goods that could be traded for muskets. In earlier days, each group had kept only a few prisoners of war as slaves and had used them only in menial tasks connected with cooking and burden bearing. How the guns changed this has been described in greater detail elsewhere (Vayda, 1960:106–107; Vayda, 1961b).

16. On battle mortality in the musket era, see Smith (1910*b*:17–18 and *passim*); J. Rutherford, MS, cited in Binney (1969:149, Note 30); and the sources cited in Vayda (1960:86). An old Maori who had been active in fighting since the 1770s gave the following description of proceedings in the case of routs in pre-musket times:

    " . . . when once the enemy broke and commenced to run, the combatants being so close together, a fast runner would knock a dozen on the head in a short time; and the great aim of these fast-running warriors . . . was to chase straight on and never stop, only striking one blow at one man, so as to cripple him, so that those behind should be sure to overtake and finish him. It was not uncommon for one man, strong and swift of foot, when the enemy were fairly routed, to stab with a light spear ten or a dozen men in such a way as to ensure their being overtaken and killed" (Maning, 1876:147–148).

17. Various estimates are cited in Lewthwaite (1950:42–43). See also Pool, 1964:226; Thompson, 1859:I; 261; Wright, 1959:102.

18. Wright's book (1959), which is an invaluable secondary source on almost all aspects of the European impact on the Maoris before 1840, includes a chapter on "The Maori Conversion"; see also Binney, 1969; Buck, 1949:524; Carleton, 1948:178; Williams, 1867:89 ff., 267–268, and *passim*.

19. On the wars between Maoris and European settlers and on the origins of these wars, see Cowan (1922–23); Dalton (1966); Sinclair (1957).

BIBLIOGRAPHIES

There are four bibliographies: I. General; II. New Guinea; III. The Ibans and Maritime Southeast Asia; and IV. New Zealand. Regardless of the chapter in which they are referred to, items not dealing specifically with the regions or peoples represented by the last three bibliographies are listed in the general bibliography.

I. GENERAL

Ardrey, R. (1961). *African Genesis.* Dell, New York.

Audy, J. R. (1971). Measurement and diagnosis of health. In: P. Shepard and D. McKinley, eds., *Environ/Mental: Essays on the Planet as a Home,* Houghton Mifflin, Boston.

Bateson, G. (1972). *Steps to an Ecology of Mind.* Chandler, San Francisco.

Birdsell, J. B. (1957). Some population problems involving Pleistocene man. *Cold Spring Harbor Symposia on Quantitative Biology* **22**:47–68.

Bohannan, P. (1954). The migration and expansion of the Tiv. *Africa* **24**:2–16.

Bremer, S., Singer, J. D., and Luterbacher, U. (1973). The population density and war proneness of European nations, 1816–1965. *Comparative Political Studies* **6**:329–348.

Carroll, B. A. (1970). War termination and conflict theory: Value premises, theories, and policies. *American Academy of Political and Social Science, Annals* **392**:14–29.

Colinvaux, P. (1973). *Introduction to Ecology*. Wiley, New York.

Collins, P. W., and Vayda, A. P. (1969). Functional analysis and its aims. *Australian and New Zealand Journal of Sociology* **5**:153–156.

Converse, E. (1968). The war of all against all: A review of *The Journal of Conflict Resolution, 1957–1958. Journal of Conflict Resolution* **12**:471–532.

Cook, S. F. (1972). *Prehistoric Demography*, McCaleb Module in Anthropology No. 16. Addison-Wesley Modular Publications, Reading.

Cowgill, G. (1975). On causes and consequences of ancient and modern population changes. *American Anthropologist*, **77**:505–525.

Douglas, M. (1966). Population control in primitive groups. *British Journal of Sociology* **17**:263–273.

Dumond, D. E. (1972). Population growth and political centralization. In: B. Spooner, ed., *Population Growth: Anthropological Implications*. M.I.T. Press, Cambridge.

Fathauer, G. H. (1954). The structure and causation of Mohave warfare. *Southwestern Journal of Anthropology* **10**:97–118.

Force, D. C. (1974). Ecology of insect host–parasitoid communities. *Science* **184**:624–632.

Fürer-Haimendorf, C. von (1967). *Morals and Merit: A Study of Values and Social Controls in South Asian Societies*. University of Chicago Press, Chicago.

Fürer-Haimendorf, C. von (1969). *The Konyak Nagas, an Indian Frontier Tribe*. Holt, Rinehart & Winston, New York.

Gibson, C. (1952). *Tlaxcala in the Sixteenth Century*. Yale University Press, New Haven.

Hallpike, C. R. (1973). Functionalist interpretations of primitive warfare. *Man* **8**:451–470.

Harris, M. (1968). *The Rise of Anthropological Theory*. Crowell, New York.

Harris, M. (1971). *Culture, Man, and Nature*. Crowell, New York.

Harris, M. (1972). Warfare old and new. *Natural History* **81** (3):18–20.

Hempel, C. G. (1959). The logic of functional analysis. In: L. Gross, ed., *Symposium on Sociological Theory*. Row, Peterson; Evanston.

Hubbell, S. P. (1973). Populations and simple food webs as energy filters: I. One-species systems. *American Naturalist* **107**:94–121.

Hutton, J. H. (1921). *The Angami Nagas*. Macmillan , London.

Hutton, J. H. (1928). The significance of head-hunting in Assam. *Journal of the Royal Anthropological Institute* **58**:399–408.

Hutton, J. H. (1930). Head-hunting. *Man in India* **10**:207–215.

Kryzywicki, L. (1934). *Primitive Society and Its Vital Statistics*. Macmillan, London.

Lattimore, O. (1962). *Studies in Frontier History*. Oxford University Press, London.

Lesser, A. (1959). Some comments on the concept of the intermediate society. In: V. F. Ray, ed., *Proceedings of the 1959 Annual Spring Meeting of the American Ethnological Society*. American Ethnological Society, Seattle.

Lesser, A. (1961). Social fields and the evolution of society. *Southwestern Journal of Anthropology* **17**:40–48.

Lesser, A. (1968). War and the state. In M. Fried, M. Harris, and R. Murphy, eds., *War: The Anthropology of Armed Conflict and Aggression*. Natural History Press, Garden City.

Lorenz, K. (1966). *On Aggression*. Harcourt, Brace & World, New York.

Mackenzie, A. (1884). *History of the Relations of the Government with the Hill Tribes of the North-East Frontier of Bengal.* Home Department Press, Calcutta.

Mills, J. P. (1926a). *The Ao Nagas.* Macmillan, London.

Mills, J. P. (1926b). Head-hunting in Assam. *Asia* 26:876–883, 904–907.

Mills, J. P. (1935). The Naga headhunters of Assam. *Journal of the Royal Central Asian Society* 22:418–424.

Mills, J. P. (1937). *The Rengma Nagas.* Macmillan, London.

Montagu, A., ed. (1973). *Man and Aggression* (2nd ed.), Oxford University Press, London.

Montgomery, E. (1973). Ecological aspects of health and disease in local populations. *Annual Review of Anthropology* 2:31–35.

Murphy, R. F. (1964). Social change and acculturation. *New York Academy of Sciences, Transactions,* Ser. II, 26:845–854.

Murphy, R. F. (1970). Basin ethnography and ecological theory. In: E. H. Swanson, Jr., ed., *Languages and Cultures of Western North America,* Idaho State University Press, Pocatello.

Naroll, R., and Divale, W. T. (n.d.). Natural selection in cultural evolution: Warfare versus peaceful diffusion. *American Ethnologist,* in press.

Newcomb, W. W., Jr. (1950). A re-examination of the causes of Plains warfare. *American Anthropologist* 52:317–330.

Numelin, R. (1950). *The Beginnings of Diplomacy.* Ejnar Munksgaard, Copenhagen.

Powell, P. W. (1952). *Soldiers, Indians & Silver: The Northward Advance of New Spain, 1550–1600.* University of California Press, Berkeley.

Pruitt, D. G., and Snyder, R. C., eds. (1969). *Theory and Research on the Causes of War,* Prentice-Hall, Englewood Cliffs.

Rappaport, R. A. (1974). Energy and the structure of adaptation. Presented at the 140th Annual Meeting of the American Association for the Advancement of Science, San Francisco. Publication forthcoming.

Sargent, F., II (1966). Ecological implications of individuality in the context of the concept of adaptive strategy. *International Journal of Biometeorology* 10:305–322.

Sauvy, A. (1969). *General Theory of Population.* Basic Books, New York.

Scott, J. G., assisted by Hardiman, J. P. (1900). *Gazetteer of Upper Burma and the Shan States,* Part 1, Vol. 1. Government Printing, Rangoon.

Scudder, T. (1973). The human ecology of big projects: River basin development and resettlement. *Annual Review of Anthropology* 2:45–55.

Shakespear, L. W. (1914). *History of Upper Assam, Upper Burmah and North-Eastern Frontier.* Macmillan, London.

Simpson, G. G. (1949). *The Meaning of Evolution.* Yale University Press, New Haven.

Slobodkin, L. B. (1968). Toward a predictive theory of evolution. In: R. C. Lewontin, ed., *Population Biology and Evolution.* Syracuse University Press, Syracuse.

Slobodkin, L. B. (1974). Mind, bind, and ecology: A review of Gregory Bateson's collected essays. *Human Ecology* 2:67–74.

Slobodkin, L. B. (MS). The peculiar evolutionary strategy of man. Unpublished paper.

Slobodkin, L. B., and Rapoport, A. (1974). An optimal strategy of evolution. *Quarterly Review of Biology* 49:181–200.

Smith, P. E. L., and Young, T. C., Jr. (1972). The evolution of early agriculture and culture in Greater Mesopotamia: A trial model. In: B. Spooner, ed., *Population Growth: Anthropological Implications*. M.I.T. Press, Cambridge.

Stevens, S. (1971). The "rat packs" of New York. *New York Times Magazine*, November 28, pp. 28–29, 91–95.

Steward, J. H., and Shimkin, D. B. (1962). Some mechanisms of sociocultural evolution. In: H. Hoagland and R. Burhoe, eds., *Evolution and Man's Progress*. Columbia University Press, New York.

Stinchcombe, A. L. (1968). *Constructing Social Theories*. Harcourt, Brace & World, New York.

Street, J. M. (1969). An evaluation of the concept of carrying capacity. *Professional Geographer* 21:104–107.

Thompson, W. S. (1929). *Danger Spots in World Population*. Knopf, New York.

Vayda, A. P. (1961). Expansion and warfare among swidden agriculturalists. *American Anthropologist* 63:346–358.

Vayda, A. P. (1967). Research on the functions of primitive war. *Peace Research Society (International), Papers* 7:133–138.

Vayda, A. P. (1974). Warfare in ecological perspective. *Annual Review of Ecology and Systematics* 5:183–193.

Vayda, A. P., and Rappaport, R. A. (1968). Ecology, cultural and noncultural. In: J. A. Clifton, ed., *Introduction to Cultural Anthropology*. Houghton Mifflin, Boston.

Wilkinson, R. G. (1973a). *Poverty and Progress: An Ecological Perspective on Economic Development*. Praeger, New York.

Wilkinson, R. G. (1973b). Progress to poverty. *Ecologist* 3:342–347.

Wolf, E. R. (1955). Types of Latin American peasantry : A preliminary discussion. *American Anthropologist* 57:452–471.

Wright, Q. (1965). *A Study of War* (2nd ed.), University of Chicago Press, Chicago.

Wynne-Edwards, V. C. (1962). *Animal Dispersion in Relation to Social Behaviour*. Oliver and Boyd, Edinburgh.

II. NEW GUINEA

Attenborough, D. (1960). *Quest in Paradise*. Lutterworth Press, London.

Baal, J. van (1966). *Dema: Description and Analysis of Marind-Anim Culture (South New Guinea)*. Martinus Nijhoff, The Hague.

Brookfield, H. C. (1962). Local study and comparative method: An example from central New Guinea. *Association of American Geographers, Annals* 52:242–254.

Brookfield, H. C., and Brown, P. (1963). *Struggle for Land*. Oxford University Press, Melbourne.

Buchbinder, G. (1973). *Maring Microadaptation: A Study of Demographic, Genetic and Phenotypic Variation among the Simbai Valley Maring of Australian New Guinea*. Unpublished Ph.D. dissertation in anthropology, Columbia University, New York.

Bunn, G., and Scott, G. (1962). *Languages of the Mount Hagen Sub-district*. The Summer Institute of Linguistics, Ukarumpa, Eastern Highlands, Territory of New Guinea.

Clarke, W. C. (1966). From extensive to intensive shifting cultivation: A succession from New Guinea. *Ethnology* 5:347–359.

Clarke, W. C. (1971). *Place and People: An Ecology of a New Guinean Community.* University of California Press, Berkeley.

Cook, E. A. (1967). *Manga Social Organization.* Unpublished Ph. D. dissertation in anthropology, Yale University, New Haven.

Hallpike, C. R. (1973). Functionalist interpretations of primitive warfare. *Man* 8:451–470.

Koch, K.-F. (1974). *War and Peace in Jalémó: The Management of Conflict in Highland New Guinea.* Harvard University Press, Cambridge.

Lowman, C. (1973). *Displays of Power: Art and War among the Marings of New Guinea.* Museum of Primitive Art, New York.

Lowman-Vayda, C. (1968). Maring Big Men. *Anthropological Forum* 2:199–243.

McCarthy, F. D. (1959). Head-hunters of Oceania. *Australian Museum Magazine* 13:76–80.

Meggitt, M. J. (1957a). Enga political organization: A preliminary description. *Mankind* 5:133–137.

Meggitt, M. J. (1957b). The Ipili of the Porgera valley, Western Highlands District, Territory of New Guinea. *Oceania* 28:31–55.

Meggitt, M. J. (1962). Growth and decline of agnatic descent groups among the Mae Enga of the New Guinea highlands. *Ethnology* 1:158–165.

Meggitt, M. J. (1965). *The Lineage System of the Mae-Enga of New Guinea.* Oliver and Boyd, Edinburgh.

Meggitt, M. J. (1972). System and subsystem: The Te exchange cycle among the Mae Enga. *Human Ecology* 1:111–123.

Rappaport, R. A. (1967). *Pigs for the Ancestors: Ritual in the Ecology of a New Guinea People.* Yale University Press, New Haven.

Rappaport , R. A. (1969). Population dispersal and land redistribution among the Maring of New Guinea. In: D. Damas, ed., *Ecological Essays,* National Museum of Canada Bulletin No. 230, National Museum of Canada, Ottawa.

Salisbury, R. F. (1963). Ceremonial economics and political equilibrium. In: *VIe Congrès International des Sciences Anthropologiques et Ethnologiques, II. Ethnologie,* Vol. 1. Musée de l'Homme, Paris.

Souter, G. (1964). *New Guinea: The Last Unknown.* Angus and Robertson, Sydney.

Street, J. M. (1969). An evaluation of the concept of carrying capacity. *Professional Geographer* 21:104–107.

Street, J. M. (n.d.). Soil conservation by shifting cultivators in the Bismarck Mountains of New Guinea. Unpublished paper.

Vayda, A. P. (1967). Research on the functions of primitive war. *Peace Research Society (International), Papers* 7:133–138.

Vayda, A. P. (1972). Pigs. In: *Encyclopaedia of Papua and New Guinea,* Vol. 2. Melbourne University Press, Melbourne.

Vayda, A. P., and Cook, E. A. (1964). Structural variability in the Bismarck Mountain cultures of New Guinea: A preliminary report. *New York Academy of Sciences, Transactions* 26:798–803.

Vayda, A. P., Leeds, A., and Smith, D. B. (1961). The place of pigs in Melanesian subsistence. In: V. E. Garfield, ed., *Proceedings of the 1961 Annual Spring Meeting of the American Ethnological Society.* University of Washington Press, Seattle.

Vial, L. G. (1942). They fight for fun. *Walkabout* 9 (1):5–9.

Watson, J. B. (1970). Society as organized flow: The Tairora case. *Southwestern Journal of Anthropology* **26**:107–124.
Wurm, S. A., and Laycock, D. C. (1961). The question of language and dialect in New Guinea. *Oceania* **32**:128–143.

III. THE IBANS AND MARITIME SOUTHEAST ASIA

Anonymous [J. Crawfurd?] (1825). Malay pirates. *Asiatic Journal* 19 (March):243–245 (regarded by Tarling [1963:28] as probably of Crawfurd's authorship).
Baring-Gould, S., and Bampfylde, C. A. (1909). *A History of Sarawak under Its Two White Rajahs.* Henry Sotheran, London.
Beccari, O. (1904). *Wanderings in the Great Forests of Borneo.* Archibald Constable, London.
Brooke, C. (1866). *Ten Years in Sarawak,* 2 vols. Tinsley Brothers, London.
Brown, D. E. (1970). *The Structure and History of a Bornean Malay Sultanate.* Monograph of the Brunei Museum Journal, Vol. 2, No. 2.
Chamerovzow, L. A. [1851]. *Borneo Facts versus Borneo Fallacies.* Charles Gilpin [London].
Crawfurd, J. (1820). *History of the Indian Archipelago.* Archibald Constable, Edinburgh.
Dampier, W. (1968). *A New Voyage round the World.* Dover, New York.
Devereux, H. B. (1855). Memorandum on the piracy of the Serebas and Sakarran Dyaks. In: *Reports,* pp. 21–28. (See reference below.)
Earl, G. W. (1837). *The Eastern Seas.* William Hallen, London.
Forrest, T. (1780). *A Voyage to New Guinea and the Moluccas from Balambangan.* G. Scott, London.
Freeman, J. D. (1955). *Iban Agriculture.* Colonial Research Studies No. 18, Her Majesty's Stationery Office, London.
Freeman, J. D. (1970). *Report on the Iban.* London School of Economics Monographs on Social Anthropology No. 41, Athlone Press, London.
Gomes, E. H. (1911). *Seventeen Years among the Sea Dayaks of Borneo.* Seeley, London.
Hornaday, W. T. (1890). *Two Years in the Jungle.* Charles Scribner's Sons, New York.
Horsburgh, Rev. A (1858). *Sketches in Borneo.* L. Russell, Anstruther.
Hose, C., and McDougall, W. (1912). *The Pagan Tribes of Borneo,* 2 vols. Macmillan, London.
Hume, J. (1853). *A Letter to the Right Honourable the Earl of Malmesbury . . . relative to the Proceedings of Sir James Brooke . . . in Borneo.* Robson, Levey, and Franklyn, London.
Irwin, G. (1955). *Nineteenth Century Borneo: A Study in Diplomatic Rivalry.* Verhandelingen van het Koninklijk Instituut voor Taal-,Land-, en Volkenkunde, part 15, Martinus Nijhoff, 's-Gravenhage.
Kennedy, R. (1942). *The Ageless Indies.* John Day, New York.
Keppel, H. (1846). *The Expedition to Borneo of H.M.S. Dido for the Suppression of Piracy: with Extracts from the Journal of James Brooke.* Harper & Brothers, New York.
Keppel, H. (1853). *A Visit to the Indian Archipelago, in H. M. Ship Maeander,* 2 vols. Richard Bentley, London.

Leach, E. (1965). The nature of war. *Disarmament and Arms Control* **3**:165–183.

Logan, J. R. (1847). The present condition of the Indian archipelago. *Journal of the Indian Archipelago and Eastern Asia* **1**:1–21.

Low, H. (1848). *Sarawak: Its Inhabitants and Productions*. Richard Bentley, London.

MacDonald, M. (1956). *Borneo People*. Clarke, Irwin & Co., Toronto.

McCarthy, F. D. (1959). Head-hunters of Oceania. *Australian Museum Magazine* **13**:76–80.

Moor, J. H., ed. (1837). *Notices of the Indian Archipelago, and Adjacent Countries*. Singapore.

Mundy, R. (1848). *Narrative of Events in Borneo and Celebes . . . from the Journals of James Brooke*, 2 vols. John Murray, London.

Pringle, R. (1970). *Rajahs and Rebels: The Ibans of Sarawak under Brooke Rule, 1841–1941*. Cornell University Press, Ithaca.

Raffles, T. S. (1821). Introduction. In: *Malay Annals: Translated from the Malay Language by the Late Dr. John Leyden*. Longman, Hurst, Rees, Orme, and Brown, London.

Reports of the Commissioners Appointed to Inquire into Certain Matters Connected with the Position of Sir James Brooke (Parliamentary Command Paper 1976) (1855). Harrison and Sons, London.

Roth, H. L. (1896). *The Natives of Sarawak and British North Borneo*, 2 vols. Truslove & Hanson, London.

Runciman, S. (1960). *The White Rajahs: A History of Sarawak from 1841 to 1946*. Cambridge University Press, Cambridge.

St. John, S. (1863). *Life in the Forests of the Far East* (2nd ed.), 2 vols. Smith, Elder and Co., London.

St. John, S. (1879). *The Life of Sir James Brooke, Rajah of Sarawak*. William Blackwood and Sons, Edinburgh.

Sandin, B. (1962). *Sengalang Burong*. Borneo Literature Bureau, Kuching.

Sandin, B. (1968). *The Sea Dayaks of Borneo before White Rajah Rule*. Michigan State University Press, Glasgow (printed in Great Britain by Robert Maclehose and Co.).

Smythies, B. E. (1949). To-morrow to fresh woods and pastures new. (A policy for shifting cultivation.) *Sarawak Gazette* **75**:251–255 (No. 1099, Oct. 7).

Sopher, D. E. (1965). *The Sea Nomads: A Study Based on the Literature of the Maritime Boat People of Southeast Asia*. Memoirs of the National Museum (Singapore), No. 5.

Tarling, N. (1963). *Piracy and Politics in the Malay World*. F. W. Cheshire, Melbourne.

Templer, J. C., ed. (1853). *The Private Letters of Sir James Brooke, K.C.B., Rajah of Sarawak, Narrating the Events of His Life, from 1838 to the Present Time*, 3 vols. Richard Bentley, London.

Vayda, A. P. (1961a). Expansion and warfare among swidden agriculturalists. *American Anthropologist* **63**:346–358.

IV. NEW ZEALAND

The following abbreviations are used:
JPS, Journal of the Polynesian Society.
TPNZI, Transactions and Proceedings of the New Zealand Institute.

Acheson, F. O. V. (1931). Maori land customs and education: Their inter-relation. In: P. M. Jackson, ed., *Maori and Education.* Ferguson and Osborn, Wellington.

Beaglehole, E. (1940). The Polynesian Maori. In: I. L. G. Sutherland, ed., *The Maori People Today.* N. Z. Inst. of Internatl. Affairs and N. Z. Council for Educ. Research, Wellington.

Best, E. (1924). *The Maori,* 2 vols. Polynesian Society Memoir No. 5. Board of Maori Ethnological Research, Wellington.

Binney, J. (1968). Christianity and the Maoris to 1840: A comment. *New Zealand Journal of History* **3**:143–165.

Buck, P. H. (Te Rangi Hiroa) (1924). The passing of the Maori. *TPNZI* **55**:362–375.

Buck, P. H. (1949). *The Coming of the Maori.* Whitcombe and Tombs, Wellington.

Buick, T. L. (1911). *An Old New Zealander or, Te Rauparaha, the Napoleon of the South.* Whitcombe and Tombs, London.

Busby, J. (1832). *Authentic Information Relative to New South Wales, and New Zealand.* Cross, London.

Carleton, H. (1948). *The Life of Henry Williams, Archdeacon of Wainate,* edited and revised by J. Elliott. A. H. & A. W. Reed, Wellington.

Cook, J. (1967). *The Journals of Captain James Cook on His Voyages of Discovery,* Vol. 3,*The Voyage of the 'Resolution' and Discovery' 1776–1780,* Part 1, J. C. Beaglehole, ed. Cambridge University Press for the Hakluyt Society, Cambridge.

Cowan, J. (1922–23). *The New Zealand Wars and the Pioneering Period,* 2 vols. Government Printer, Wellington.

Cumberland, K. B. (1949). Aotearoa Maori: New Zealand about 1780. *Geographical Review* **39**:401–424.

Dalton, B. J. (1966). A new look at the Maori wars of the sixties. *Historical Studies, Australia and New Zealand* **12**:230–247.

Earle, A. (1832). *A Narrative of a Nine Months' Residence in New Zealand in 1827.* Longman *et al.,* London.

Firth, R. (1929). *Primitive Economics of the New Zealand Maori.* George Routledge and Sons, London.

Firth, R. (1959). *Economics of the New Zealand Maori* (2nd ed. of Firth, 1929). Government Printer, Wellington.

Gudgeon, T. W. (1885). *The History and Doings of the Maoris, from the Year 1820 to . . . 1840.* Brett, Auckland.

Gudgeon, W. E. (1904). The toa taua or warrior. *JPS* **13**:238–264.

Hall, F. (1823). Extracts from the journal of Mr. Francis Hall. In: *Missionary Register for MDCCCXXIII.* L. B. Seeley and Son, London.

Hamlin, J. (1842). On the mythology of the New Zealanders. *Tasmanian Journal* **1**:254–264, 342–358.

Johansen, J. P. (1954). *The Maori and His Religion in Its Non-Ritualistic Aspects.* Ejnar Munksgaard, Copenhagen.

Kelly, L. G. (1938). Fragments of Ngapuhi history. *JPS* **47**:163–181.

Kelly, L. G. (1949). *Tainui: The Story of Hoturoa and His Descendants,* Polynesian Society Memoir No. 25. Polynesian Society, Wellington.

Lesson, R. P. (1839). *Voyage autour du monde entrepris par ordre du gouvernement sur la corvette La Coquille,* 2 vols. Pourrat Frères, Paris.

Lewthwaite, G. (1950). The population of Aotearoa: Its number and distribution. *New Zealand Geographer* **6**:35–52.

Maning, F. E. (1876). *Old New Zealand, a Tale of the Good Old Times; and a History of the War in the North Against the Chief Heke, in the Year 1845*. Richard Bentley and Son, London.

Marsden, S. (1932). *The Letters and Journals of Samuel Marsden 1765–1838*, John Rawson Elder, ed. Coulls, Somerville, Wilkie; Dunedin.

Nicholas, J. L. (1817). *Narrative of a Voyage to New Zealand Performed in the Years 1814 and 1815, in Company with the Rev. Samuel Marsden*, 2 vols. Black, London.

Polack, J. S. (1838). *New Zealand: Being a Narrative of Travels and Adventures During a Residence in the Country between the Years 1831 and 1837*, 2 vols. Bentley, London.

Pool, D. I. (1964). *The Maori Population of New Zealand*. Unpublished Ph.D. dissertation, Australian National University, Canberra.

Savage, J. (1939). *Savage's Account of New Zealand in 1805*, A. D. McKinlay, ed. Watkins, London.

Shortland, E. (1856). *Traditions and Superstitions of the New Zealanders* (2nd ed.). Longman *et al.*, London.

Sinclair, K. (1957). *The Origins of the Maori Wars*. New Zealand University Press, Wellington.

Smith, N. (1942). *Native Custom and Law Affecting Native Land*. Maori Purposes Fund Board, Wellington.

Smith, S. P. (1896–97). *The Peopling of the North: Notes on the Ancient Maori History of the Northern Peninsula and Sketches of the History of the Ngati-Whatua Tribe of Kaipara, New Zealand: "Heru-Kapanga."* JPS 6–7, Supplement.

Smith, S. P. (1910a). *History and Traditions of the Maoris of the West Coast, North Island of New Zealand Prior to 1840*, Polynesian Society Memoir No. 1. Polynesian Society, New Plymouth.

Smith, S. P. (1910b). *Maori Wars of the Nineteenth Century*. Whitcombe and Tombs, Christchurch.

Tapp, E. J. (1958). *Early New Zealand, a Dependency of New South Wales 1788–1841*. Melbourne University Press, Melbourne.

Thomson, A. S. (1859). *The Story of New Zealand*, 2 vols. Murray, London.

Travers, W. T. L. (1872). The life and times of Te Rauparaha. *TPNZI* 5:19–93.

Tregear, E. (1904). *The Maori Race*. Willis, Wanganui.

Urlich, D. U. (1970). The introduction and diffusion of firearms in New Zealand 1800–1840. *JPS* **79**:399–410.

Vayda, A. P. (1960). *Maori Warfare*, Polynesian Society Maori Monographs, No. 2. Polynesian Society, Wellington.

Vayda, A. P. (1961a). Expansion and warfare among swidden agriculturalists. *American Anthropologist* **63**:346–358.

Vayda, A. P. (1961b). Maori prisoners and slaves in the nineteenth century. *Ethnohistory* **8**:144–155.

Vennel, C. W. (1967). *The Brown Frontier: New Zealand Historical Stories and Studies 1806–1877*. A. H. and A. W. Reed, Wellington.

Walsh, Archdeacon P. (1907). The passing of the Maori. *TPNZI* **40**:154–175.

White, J. (1974). *Te Rou; or the Maori at Home. A Tale, Exhibiting the Social Life, Manners, Habits, and Customs of the Maori Race in New Zealand prior to the Introduction of Civilization Amongst Them*. Low, London.

White, J. (1885). Maori customs and superstitions, being the subject of two lectures delivered at the Mechanics' Institute, in Auckland, during the year 1861. In: T.

W. Gudgeon, *The History and Doings of the Maoris, from the Year 1820 to . . . 1840.* Brett, Auckland.

White, J. (1887–90). *The Ancient History of the Maori.* 6 vols. Government Printer, Wellington.

Williams, Rev. W. (1867). *Christianity among the New Zealanders.* Seeley, Jackson, and Halliday, London.

Wright, H. M. (1959). *New Zealand, 1769–1840: Early Years of Western Contact.* Harvard University Press, Cambridge.

Yate, Rev. W. (1835). *An Account of New Zealand.* Seeley J. Burnside, London.

INDEX